LEARNING MINDSET FOR LEADERS

Leveraging Experience to Accelerate Development

Steve Terrell, Ed.D.

Revised March 21, 2021

Table of Contents

Learning Mindset for Leaders

FIRST THINGS FIRST: GUIDE TO USING THIS BOOK

This book presents the Learning Mindset model, a framework for **L**everaging **E**xperience to **A**ccelerate **D**evelopment (**LEAD**), and provides a robust collection of developmental tools and resources to help leaders increase their Learning Mindset and Learning Practices. We strongly believe that leaders who have a Learning Mindset experience more growth and development than leaders who do not have this attitude toward experience and learning. The book was written to help everyone who reads it – leaders, managers, executive coaches, and leadership development practitioners – to increase their understanding of how to learn from experience. The book is research-based yet imminently practical, with many activities that anyone can use in day-to-day life and work. We recommend a specific sequence of activities, found on the next few pages, to make the most of the model and tools. But first, let's get oriented to the contents and organization of the book before you go further.

The **Introduction** describes the business dynamics and conditions that make a Learning Mindset so important for leaders. The model is grounded in the real world, where unexpected problems and constant change test leaders in ways they haven't experienced before. Responding effectively to these challenges means that leaders must always exercise a strong Learning Mindset.

The **Learning Mindset Overview** presents the Learning Mindset model and discusses how it enables leaders to learn more from experience. Leaders with a strong Learning Mindset are oriented to learn from every experience they engage in. Their high level of curiosity and drive to learn leads them to demonstrate certain behaviors that we call "Learning Practices," the actual "how to" of learning from experience.

The **Learning Practices** section presents a detailed description of ten "Learning Practices," actions that leaders take to accelerate and enhance your learning from experience. We don't focus on training programs, conferences, or other traditional learning approaches to promote development as leaders. Instead, we believe that time on the job represents your best and most accessible opportunity to learn: from your day-to-day experience. We give you the tools and skills to actually learn from your on-the-job experiences, unlike most other approaches to leadership development.

The **Developmental Roadmap** lays out our recommended sequence of activities for you to follow, in order to get the most from this book. It may not fit your preferences, so by all means find your own way through if our recommendations don't work for you.

In the **Tools and Resources** section of the book you will find the Learning Mindset Questionnaire (LMQ) and the Learning Practices Inventory (LPS), with instructions on how to use them to assist your development. Following these self-assessments we provide guidance on taking action to learn more from experience and a Development Action Plan template to plot your path forward.

Finally, an extensive **Recommended Reading** list of articles and books related to learning from experience provides you with additional resources to support your development.

Learning Mindset for Leaders

"Expertise at learning has become the key capability necessary for survival, success and fulfillment."
David A. Kolb & Bauback Yeganeh

INTRODUCTION

Adaptive challenges, complex problems, volatile business environments – increasingly these are just some of the circumstances business leaders find themselves in, placing unprecedented demands on their capabilities to be effective. After a period of faltering corporate performance IBM Chief Executive Virginia Rometty put the entire company on notice, telling employees "Where we haven't transformed rapidly enough, we struggled. We have to step up with that and deal with that, and that is on all levels." (Wall Street Journal, April 24, 2013) Undoubtedly, IBM is not alone in the struggle to keep up with the challenges of changing markets and conditions. Many organizations today are operating in an environment characterized by Volatility, Uncertainty, Complexity, and Ambiguity (VUCA[1]), and as a result their leaders are likely struggling with major challenges they have never had to deal with before. Effectively responding to these challenges means that today's organizations "demand a 'Learning-Integrated Life' – where individuals are always in a learning mindset."[2] Leaders must be able to quickly size up people and situations, make tough decisions and take appropriate action without complete information, and flexibly change on the fly in order to produce results in new, demanding, first-time situations.

---

[1] Volatility, uncertainty, complexity, and ambiguity. Wikipedia article, sourced January 30, 2020.
[2] *The Future of Lifelong Learning – Designing for a Learning-Integrated Life.* D2L Corporation, 2020.

Succeeding in such conditions requires leaders to actively and intentionally learn from their day-to-day experience. They must apply what they are learning to new challenging situations, and continue learning as they go forward. Unfortunately, the ability to learn from experience is a capability that many leaders either take for granted or ignore outright. However, the leaders who consistently practice the skills and tactics of learning from experience are significantly better equipped to deal with the complexities and challenges of modern business life.

LEARNING MINDSET OVERVIEW

"The ability to learn is a defining characteristic of being human; the ability to continue learning is an essential skill of leadership. When leaders lose that ability, they inevitably falter." Warren Bennis and Robert Thomas

"Experience is the best teacher." How many times have we heard that, or said it ourselves? When it comes to developing as a leader, it is widely held that experience is a central component. Unfortunately, having an experience does not guarantee learning from it. Many people do not learn from experience, because they lack the knowledge and skills needed to do so. Research has shown that providing opportunities and challenging assignments to leaders doesn't automatically result in their development. A study by Fiedler[3] actually found that longer leader tenure and experience was negatively correlated with team performance. Many leadership and learning theorists have found that learning from experience is not a passive process, but requires an approach to living that makes learning one's primary and most important focus. It may be true that experience is the best teacher,

---

[3] Fiedler, F. E. (1970). Leadership experience and leader performance: Another hypothesis shot to hell. Organizational Behavior and Human Performance(5), 1-14.

but only for those who actively utilize specific learning strategies and skills to derive the lessons of experience.

The problem is that most of us live our lives on "automatic pilot," making little or no effort to learn from our experiences. Have you ever gone through your workday, running from meeting to meeting, and suddenly discovered that the day is over and you don't recall anything you did or said? We all develop patterns or habits of behavior that make it easier and simpler to go through life, without having to think about things every single time. This phenomenon is called "automaticity," when you can perform a skill without having to consciously think about it. However, this also hurts us because it leads to our sleepwalking through valuable experiences that hold hidden learning, if only we could notice! The speed of business makes it extremely difficult to break the habit patterns that we use to move at pace through our workdays. If we assume that learning happens automatically and give little thought or energy to learning or improving our learning capability, then we miss out on opportunities to learn, grow, and develop as leaders.

To get the most out of your day-to-day experiences, focus on enacting a **Learning Mindset** and the **Learning Practices** that follow. These two elements of learning from experience go hand in hand: from a Learning Mindset (attitude) emerge Learning Practices (actions).

What is "Learning Mindset"?

Think of a mindset as a habitual or characteristic mental attitude that determines how you will interpret and respond to situations. In the context of learning from experience, a Learning Mindset is an attitude that predisposes you to be open to new experiences, to believe you can and will learn, and to intentionally grow and develop from your experience. It includes the set of assumptions and beliefs that govern how you think about and approach experience and

opportunities, and whether you generally see them as opportunities to learn and develop, as well as

your typical affective stance toward learning, your emotional state or feeling about learning,

learning situations, and new experiences.

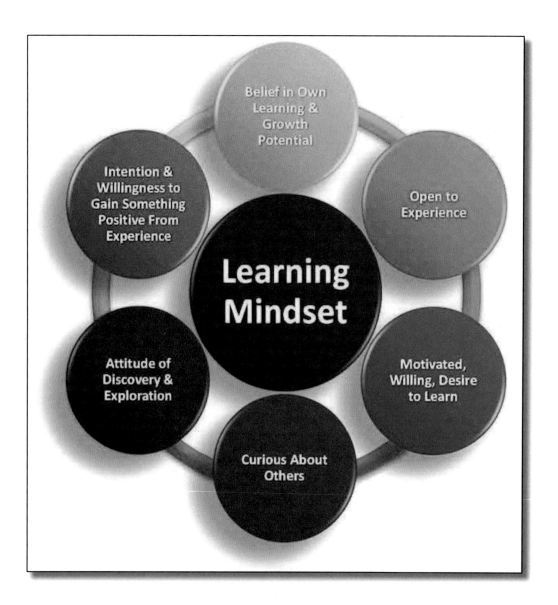

Leaders who have a Learning Mindset see opportunities to learn in all aspects of their
work life and tend to learn more than those who are closed to learning.

~ THE LEARNING MINDSET MODEL ~

The following list of the Learning Mindset model's six dimensions and their descriptors summarizes the key aspects of the model.

1. **Open to Experience**
   - Open to new experiences and ideas
   - Intellectually curious and have broad interests
   - Receptive and open to change

2. **Motivated, Willing and Desire to Change**
   - Strong internal drive and desire to learn, grow, and develop
   - Constantly seek out and engage in new experiences in order to gain new knowledge and skills
   - Enjoy the challenge and novelty of new experiences

3. **Curious About Others**
   - Feel a powerful inner need to learn about people in other countries and other parts of the world
   - Have a strong desire to understand the challenges other face and how they deal with the challenges
   - Always searching for deeper understanding about the unique ways people in diverse settings and situations (e.g. roles, organizations, cultures) behave

4. **Attitude of Discovery and Exploration**
   - Frequently seek out new, different situations in order to learn something new
   - Often strike out into unfamiliar territory just for the adventure and enjoyment of experiencing something different
   - Frequently discard old habits of mind and perceptions in order to view experiences with a fresh perspective

5. **Intention and Willingness to Gain Something Positive from Experience**
   - Act with purpose and intention to learn something from every experience I have
   - Even when an experience appears to be "negative" I search for meaning and value in the experience
   - Typically look at unsatisfying/difficult situations as opportunities to gain valuable lessons and insights from experience

6. **Belief in My Own Learning and Growth Potential**
   - Believe I am able to significantly grow and develop my knowledge, skills, and abilities
   - Believe I can substantially change how much talent I have
   - Always striving to gain new knowledge, develop new skills, and improve my abilities

It's helpful to think of Learning Mindset as a set of prescription eyeglasses or lenses through which you view the world and your experience. If you operate with a mindset that leads you to view work projects or tasks *only* as things that you need to do in order to fulfill your job responsibilities and to succeed, then you will most likely focus *only* on producing the desired results "on time and under budget," using your current knowledge and skills to accomplish the goal. Now, these are good things to achieve. But operating with a Learning Mindset leads you to view those same work projects and tasks as opportunities to learn something new while achieving the desired outcomes. As a result, you will focus *both* on expanding your current knowledge and skills *and* taking creative action to produce the desired results. The conceptual lens of Learning Mindset leads you to see every experience as an opportunity to learn, grow, and develop.

Leaders who have a **Learning Mindset** see opportunities to learn in all aspects of their work life, and tend to learn more than those who are closed to learning. According to research conducted at the University of Virginia, "Managers with a 'learning mindset' are characterized by a continuous sense of ongoing learning and transformation and receive the highest job performance ratings of all those studied."[4] And, in an article published by Harvard Business Review online, Gottfredson and Reina point out that "A learning mindset involves being motivated toward increasing one's competence and mastering something new…. Leaders with a learning mindset, compared to those with a performance mindset, are more mentally primed to increase their competence, engage in

---

[4] L.A. Isabella and T. Forbes, "Managerial Mindsets Research Project: Executive Summary," Darden Graduate School of Business Administration, University of Virginia, Charlottesville, April 1994; and interview with the authors, 13 June 1994.

deep-level learning strategies, seek out feedback, and exert more of an effort. They are also

persistent, adaptable, willing to cooperate, and tend to perform at a higher level."[5]

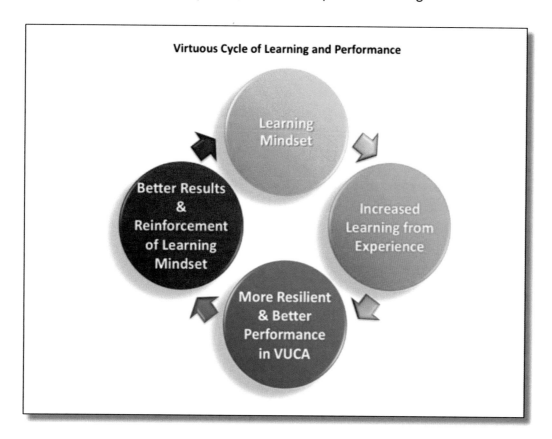

In essence, fully embracing and enacting a Learning Mindset creates a "virtuous cycle" of

learning and performance. The terms "virtuous cycle" and "vicious cycle" refer to "complex chains

of events that reinforce themselves through a feedback loop."[6] A virtuous cycle generates favorable,

or positive, results, while a vicious cycle produces detrimental results. The Learning Mindset creates

this virtuous cycle because it enables leaders to learn more from their experiences, which in turn

[5] Ryan Gottfredson and Chris Reina, "To Be a Great Leader, You Need the Right Mindset." Harvard Business Review digital article, January 17, 2020.
[6] Virtuous circle and vicious circle. Wikipedia, sourced January 30, 2020.
https://en.wikipedia.org/wiki/Virtuous_circle_and_vicious_circle

results in leaders being more resilient and performing better in VUCA conditions. This leads to achievement of better results and reinforces the importance and value of the Learning Mindset.

Our research has led us to conclude that leaders who have a Learning Mindset demonstrate an attitude or stance toward learning that embodies openness to experience; are motivated, willing, and desire to learn; are highly curious about others and how they do what they do; possess an attitude of discovery and exploration; and show an intention and willingness to gain something positive from experience. As a result of this powerful constellation of learning-related attributes, these leaders experience more growth and development than leaders who do not have this attitude toward learning.

Additionally, their Learning Mindset leads them to consistently and intentionally demonstrate certain behaviors – "Learning Practices" – so that they are constantly seeking to learn from experience in every situation, and naturally apply what they learn in new, emerging experiences. You can accelerate your own development as a leader by applying the Learning Practices in your own life and work.

Do YOU have a Learning Mindset?

Take a few minutes to explore that question by completing the <u>Learning Mindset Questionnaire</u>, found in the Tools and Resources section.

THE LEARNING PRACTICES

"What can I do to 'get better' as a leader?" This is a question that leaders frequently ask after receiving 360-degree feedback or attending a training program. It's one thing to know that you need to "think more strategically" or improve at "giving performance feedback and coaching" to your direct reports. It's something completely different to translate that down to practical actions that you can take to bring about lasting change, growth, and development.

Learning Practices are actions you can take to accelerate and enhance your learning from experience. Your actions determine whether you proactively pursue learning in your day-to-day work life or focus only on getting the job done. Since most of us spend over 90% of our work time working, not in training programs or workshops, time on the job represents our best and most accessible opportunity to learn: from our day-to-day experience. We just need to know how to use our experience to grow and develop.

Most executives focus only on doing their jobs, producing results, and don't *consciously, proactively* learn from your work experience. Given that, any learning that takes place is accidental, incidental, serendipitous, and frequently understood or implied without being stated. Even worse, some potential learning is left on the table due to neglect or failure to mine experience for lessons learned, insights gained, or skills reinforced. The opportunity and challenge is to diversify and consistently transform daily experience into learning and development. This is where the Learning Practices come in.

Leaders who consistently, intentionally, and rigorously use the Learning Practices learn significantly more, faster while achieving better results.

My research and experience, and an extensive review of the learning and leadership development literature, have revealed the following ten key learning practices that have significant potential for growing and accelerating your ability to learn from experience:

1. Take responsibility for your own learning and development
2. Approach new assignments/opportunities with openness to experience and positive intention to learn
3. Seek and use feedback
4. Develop a clear understanding of your strengths and areas of development

5. Ask great questions and demonstrate curiosity
6. Listen transformatively (intently, deeply, empathically)
7. Respond to experience with adaptability and flexibility
8. Actively reflect and practice mindfulness
9. Actively experiment with new approaches to learning
10. Closely observe and learn from others

The Learning Practices can be used in:

- Day-to-day work and life experience

- Assignments, projects, developmental opportunities

- Leadership development programs, to help leaders become better learners and better leaders

- Action Learning programs, to equip participants with knowledge, skills, and tools to learn from experience

- Coaching, to help coachees to become better learners and leaders, and to learn more, faster from experience

As you face the challenges of leading in today's world of increasing complexity, rapid change, and rising uncertainty, remember that the most effective leaders have the ability to transform their experiences into on-going growth and development. And the greater the challenge, the more significant is the opportunity to develop as a leader. If you have a *Learning Mindset* and consistently, intentionally, and rigorously put the *Learning Practices* into action, you will learn significantly more, faster, and as a result you'll perform at a higher level and create greater value for your company and for yourself.

TEN LEARNING PRACTICES

The following list of the ten Learning Practices and their descriptors (behaviors, behavioral trends and patterns, and tendencies) is provided as an overview of the practices and what they look like in action.

1. **Take responsibility for your own learning and development**
   - Feel personally accountable to actively pursue your own professional growth and development
   - Take the initiative to improve your leadership capabilities
   - Develop goals and action plans to improve your knowledge and/or abilities related to your job or career
   - Intentionally reframe your experiences to view them as learning opportunities
   - Look for ways to learn something new while pursuing your work goals, assignments, and projects
   - Persistently work through difficult issues and overcome obstacles to accomplish desired changes

2. **Approach new assignments/opportunities with openness to experience and positive intention to learn**
   - Automatically think to yourself when you have a new assignment, "This is a great opportunity to learn something new"
   - Welcome assignments to projects or tasks that you have never done before
   - Look forward to different types of experiences because of the learning you might gain
   - Find something useful to learn in most experiences
   - Intentionally look for something to learn, even when an experience is difficult, challenging, or not to your liking

3. **Seek and use feedback**
   - Ask colleagues (such as your direct manager/supervisor, peers, customers, stakeholders, and/or direct reports) for feedback about your performance, behaviors, and/or competencies
   - Listen closely to the feedback you receive
   - Follow up with and thank your colleagues for giving you useful feedback
   - Listen closely to what might NOT be said (behind the words)
   - Take feedback, both positive and constructive, to heart and do your best to use it to change, grow and develop

4. **Develop a clear understanding of your strengths and areas of development**
   - Take stock of your personality characteristics, and how they influence your performance and behavior at work
   - Assess yourself against the leadership competencies in the competency model of your organization
   - Ask others to help you by sharing their perspective on your strengths and areas for further development
   - Identify your top strengths and top areas for further development

5. **Ask great questions and demonstrate curiosity**
   - Ask open-ended questions to encourage people to expand their ideas and share them with you
   - Ask probing questions in order to learn more about something
   - Frame your questions positively
   - Ask questions from the Learning Mindset, seeking to learn rather than to judge

6. **Listen transformatively**
   - Listen to others with the Learning Mindset, seeking to learn rather than to judge
   - Listen to explore your own perceptions, filters, and biases, and become aware of how they affect your behavior
   - Listen intently, deeply, empathically
   - Listen to understand both the content and the affect of the speaker
   - Listen to grasp the intentions and deeper purpose of the speaker, i.e., what they want to achieve

7. **Respond to experience with adaptability and flexibility**
   - Change your behavior according to the situation at hand
   - Resist the tendency to use "muscle memory" (old, familiar ways of leading and acting) and proactively choose my actions depending on the circumstance
   - Not insisting on your own way, even when you have "been there, done that" and think you know the "right" way
   - Soliciting others' ideas about how to handle situations, especially those from different cultural backgrounds and life experiences

8. **Actively reflect / Practice mindfulness**
   - Take the time to reflect on and think about situations you have been in at work, what your behavior was, how you were feeling, what the outcome was, and any insight or lesson you gained
   - Actively reflect during situations, so that you self-direct or self-correct and make changes to your behavior or words that bring about a more desirable outcome
   - Reflect with others to gain an appreciation for their perspective and to broaden your awareness

- Maintain a high degree of awareness of the people, actions, interactions, and dynamics around you, in order to make sense of situations and experiences as they occur
- Pay attention to the present moment; watch your thoughts with detachment and without judgment

9. **Actively experiment with new approaches to learning**
   - Frequently try different approaches to solving problems
   - Play around with different ways of presenting an idea you have
   - Brainstorm with colleagues new ways of doing what you have done for years

10. **Closely observe and learn from others**
   - Train yourself to become a better observer
   - Seek out someone who is known to be an expert at something you want to learn about, and interview them about how they learned it themselves
   - Identify someone who has a Learning Mindset and who uses many of the Learning Practices; ask them about their learning journey and how they developed their skills at learning from experience
   - Identify someone who is recognized as an outstanding leader or specialist, and "shadow" them to learn first-hand how they do what they do; interview them to learn more
   - Work with a small group of leaders to learn from them and build a supportive social network that provides both motivation and accountability for learning

Self-Assessment Tools

For each Learning Practice you will find self-assessment tools to help you evaluate your use of the Learning Practice. Carefully use the self-assessments to obtain a sense of how frequently you use specific behaviors associated with each practice and determine your overall rating for each practice. After you complete the self-assessments for each Learning Practice, thoughtfully go back through the Potential Developmental Actions provided to identify specific behaviors you can use more frequently to drive your learning from experience. Take the time to use the Reflection Questions provided at the end of each Learning Practice section as a means of gaining insight.

How strong are YOUR Learning Practices?

Take a few minutes to explore that question by completing the Learning Practices Survey, found in the Tools and Resources section.

DEVELOPMENTAL ROADMAP

So far, we've reviewed the Learning Mindset model and the Learning Practices. How do you use this information to accelerate your development as a leader? We provide a couple of approaches to using this book to move forward from here, so you can use one of them or make up your own approach. It's up to you.

One approach is to **(1)** first read through the Learning Practice chapters in sequence, completing the Self-Assessments and Reflection Questions as you go. **(2)** Next, complete the Learning Mindset Questionnaire (LMQ) and Learning Practices Survey (LPS). This approach will immerse you in each Learning Practice one at a time but it could be a chore to give each chapter the same degree of attention. However, remember that you don't know what you don't know, so neglecting or skipping over a chapter could create a blind spot. If you're not sure where you want to focus your developmental energy, this approach may give you the best results. Also, if you want to learn more about a specific topic, you'll find a wide range of articles and books to tap into in the Recommended Readings. **(3)** Finally, create your Development Action Plan to guide and focus your work toward a stronger Learning Mindset and Learning Practices.

Another approach is to **(1)** complete the Learning Mindset Questionnaire (LMQ) and Learning Practices Survey (LPS) before you **(2)** read through the Learning Practice chapters. This could help you target your chapter reading to areas where you want to focus your development time and energy. You could save some time and get to the Development Action Plan sooner, if that's important to you. The downside to this approach is that you could miss out on something where you have a blind spot or mistakenly believe that you're not in need of development. Again, if you want to learn more about a specific topic, you'll find a wide range of articles and books to tap into in the Recommended Readings. **(3)** Finally, create your Development Action Plan to guide and focus your work toward a stronger Learning Mindset and Learning Practices.

Either approach will yield positive results. The key is to take responsibility for your own growth and development and take action! To make these approaches even more practical and concrete, here is a step by step description of the action you should take to use the Learning Mindset Questionnaire, the Learning Practices Survey, and the Development Action Plan, regardless of which approach you decide to use.

Learning Mindset Questionnaire (LMQ)

1. Answer the LMQ, calculate your scores, and plot your average rating for each dimension.

2. Use the Interpretation guidelines to understand your LMQ results.

   - If your overall average rating is in either the Moderate or Opportunity range, take note of any of the 6 dimensions you rated lower than the others.

   - Make a list of the specific LM dimensions you want to increase or improve. You will address these in your LM Development Action Plan.

3. For each of the dimensions you put in your list, read and meditate on the Reflection Questions provided for the Learning Mindset model.

Learning Practices Survey (LPS)

1. Answer the LPS, calculate your scores, and plot your total rating for each learning practice.

2. Use the Interpretation guidelines to understand your LPS results.

   – If your overall average rating is in either the Moderate or Opportunity range, take note of any of the 10 learning practices you rated lower than the others.

   – Make a list of the specific learning practices you want to increase or improve. You will address these in your LM Development Action Plan.

3. For each of the learning practices you put in your list, use the relevant chapter in LM4L to increase your understanding, and read and meditate on the Reflection Questions provided for the Learning Practices.

Development Action Plan

1. Review your results and scores from the LMQ and LPS, and identify items you want to improve on.

2. Use the guidance on page 180 on how to identify these action items, and then review the Recommended Development Actions for the relevant Learning Practice or Learning Mindset dimension. Choose one or two development actions you plan to take to improve your ability to learn from experience. List the actions you plan to take in the Development Action Plan provided.

3. Periodically review your action plan and reflect on your progress.

CHAPTER ORGANIZATION

Each Learning Practice chapter of the Guide is organized around one of the ten Learning Practices. For each Practice, you will see Behaviors, Behavioral Trends and Patterns, and Tendencies associated with demonstration of the Practices. The behaviors listed for each of the Learning Practices are descriptive and are not considered a comprehensive or exhaustive list. There are many ways to demonstrate the Learning Practices needed to be effective and successful at learning from experience. This guide describes some of the most important Behaviors, Behavioral Trends and Patterns, and Tendencies – those that we believe you will find to be important to make the most of your day-to-day work experience. You may think of other Behaviors that are important to your own development and we encourage you to think through and analyze how those behaviors relate to the Learning Practices and the Learning Mindset model.

Each Learning Practice chapter is organized in the same way. Here's an example:

- **Learning Practice # and Descriptor:** "1. Take responsibility for my own learning and development"
- ***Behaviors, Behavioral Trends and Patterns, Tendencies:*** "a. Hold yourself personally accountable to actively pursue your own professional growth and development"
- **Potential Developmental Actions:** "Review your work calendar/schedule to identify how much time you invest every week into your own learning, growth, or development. List the number of hours or minutes you invested each week. . ."
- **Self-Assessment Tool:** "Score yourself on taking responsibility for your own learning and development" using the scale provided.
- **Reflection Questions:** "What have you done in the last year to take the initiative to improve your leadership capabilities?"

1. Take Responsibility for My Own Learning and Development

"Taking charge of your own learning is a part of taking charge of your own life, which is the sine qua non in becoming an integrated person."
Warren G. Bennis

Introduction

Learning Practice #1 – Taking Responsibility for My Own Learning and Development – is the initial evidence that you have a Learning Mindset, because until you actually **own** your development, **taking (not just accepting)** responsibility for your own learning and development, you are a passive by-stander, waiting or sleep-walking through your life. Until and unless you take responsibility for your own growth and development, learning may or may not happen, and if it does it will be accidental, incidental, serendipitous, and tacit. Taking responsibility means that you are in charge, you are the driving force behind your development, making things happen rather than being laissez-faire and letting things happen.

Review the list of behaviors, behavioral trends and patterns, and tendencies below. As you do, reflect on your own experience and try to recall specific situations or events that shed light on your own patterns of behavior related to this Learning Practice.

BEHAVIORS, BEHAVIORAL TRENDS AND PATTERNS, TENDENCIES:

- Feel personally accountable to actively pursue your own professional growth and development
- Take the initiative to improve your leadership capabilities
- Develop goals and action plans to improve your knowledge and/or abilities related to your job or career
- Intentionally reframe your experiences to view them as learning opportunities
- Look for ways to learn something new while pursuing your work goals, assignments, and projects
- Persistently work through difficult issues and overcome obstacles to accomplish desired changes

Potential Developmental Actions

Review the following for examples of developmental actions you can take to enhance your effectiveness as taking personal responsibility for your own learning, growth and development as a leader. Identify at least one or two actions that you will work to integrate into your day-to-day work life.

HOLD YOURSELF PERSONALLY ACCOUNTABLE TO ACTIVELY PURSUE YOUR OWN PROFESSIONAL GROWTH AND DEVELOPMENT:

- Review your work calendar/schedule to identify how much time you invest every week into your own learning, growth, or development. List the number of hours or minutes you invested each week over the past 3 months, along with the type of learning, growth, or development activity. Include activities such as workshops attended, professional books or articles read, webinars attended, etc. Decide how much time you want to invest every week, in which types of activities, and note that in your work calendar/schedule. Use this to guide your activities going forward.
- Conduct a realistic self-assessment of your leadership capabilities, and identify one area to improve. Use your organization's leadership competency model or a commercially available model (there are plenty around).
- Tell someone at work who you trust (friend, colleague/peer, direct manager) that you have decided to work on one area to improve and ask for their support.
- Tell your direct reports that you have decided to work on one area to improve and ask for their support.

TAKE THE INITIATIVE TO IMPROVE YOUR LEADERSHIP CAPABILITIES:

- Set a goal to develop a specific leadership competency that is required for your next position, not your current position. Research how you can develop that competency in your current position, through projects, assignments, or expanded responsibilities. Research how you can develop that competency in non-work activities, such as volunteering to lead a charitable organization with the specific purpose of learning and developing the leadership competency you identified.

- Volunteer to lead projects that make you uncomfortable because you have never done something that big before, or because they are out of your area of expertise. Take on projects in unfamiliar areas for the primary purpose of growing and developing new capabilities as a leader.

- Get out your calendar, or open Outlook, Google Calendar, or your usual way of organizing your time. Set aside 15 – 30 minutes every week, on the same day of the week and time of day, to reflect on yourself as a leader. Think about what actions you took during the previous week to improve your leadership capabilities. Make a list of actions you plan to take during the coming week to improve your leadership capabilities.

- Create or join a book club where you read and discuss business books related to your profession.

- Create a reading list, and assign yourself a book or periodical to read on a regular basis. Write a one-page summary of a book from which you gained something important to you, and share it with your colleagues. Engage them in a conversation about the book summary.

DEVELOP GOALS AND ACTION PLANS TO IMPROVE YOUR KNOWLEDGE AND/OR ABILITIES RELATED TO YOUR JOB OR CAREER:

- Review your most recent Performance Appraisal to identify one area that held you back or that, if you made a significant improvement in it, would substantially improve your performance and/or the perceptions of you as a leader within your organization. Set a goal and develop a plan to improve in that area so that your progress will be noticed in your next Performance Appraisal.

- When starting a new goal, assignment, or project identify the areas in which you feel most prepared and comfortable, and least prepared and comfortable. Make it a personal learning goal to learn as much as you can about the areas in which you feel least prepared and comfortable. As you learn, share what you have learned and how it impacts your view of the project with your colleagues. Ask your colleagues – peers and direct reports – how they see the area in which you feel least prepared and comfortable. Hearing how others view a challenge or idea is often a valuable way to expand your own point of view and learn something new.

INTENTIONALLY REFRAME EXPERIENCES TO VIEW THEM AS LEARNING OPPORTUNITIES:

- "Reframing" means to change the way you look at or think about something. It means to look at old problems in a new light and attack old challenges with different and more powerful tools. In the context of learning from experience it means that you consciously change the way you see a work assignment or experience, in order to view it as a learning opportunity instead of a dead end or career ender. Reframing broadens your repertoire as a leader and gives you expanded choices. This enables you to generate more creative responses to the problems you encounter in your day-to-day work life. There is always more than one way to respond to a challenge, including those assignments that you just can't seem to view as holding any value.

- For example, you may be given a new assignment that at first seems to be undesirable or even a huge problem that could never be solved. If you look at the assignment as undesirable you may be tempted to just grit your teeth and plow through it to achieve the goal and deliver the desired results, without ever considering that valuable lessons, insights, and developmental "gems" might be waiting to be discovered.

- Even if you receive an assignment or are given a dreaded "developmental opportunity" (so-called because everyone avoids that type of assignment because it is so daunting), the attitude with which you approach it has the power to shape what you gain from the experience. If you approach it with dread, anxiety, anger, or resistance, how do you think the experience will go for you? It's pretty clear that you will experience dread, anxiety, anger, and resistance, and the negative results of carrying those feelings around with you as you attempt to complete the assignment as quickly as you can, and move on. On the other hand, if you approach it with the attitude that it is an opportunity to learn, grow, and develop, how do you think the experience will go for you? Again, it's pretty clear that if you expect and look for opportunities to learn, grow, and develop you will find them in abundance.

- Here are some tips and techniques to help you reframe how you approach assignments and experiences in order to maximize your learning.
    - *Reframing questions.* View the experience from a different perspective. Ask questions about the assignment in a way that lets you examine it from a broader perspective, and identify its less-obvious aspects. An example of a reframing question is "What are the facts of this assignment/situation, and how can each of these facts be challenged?" If you apply this question to a "delivery" problem, you might find out that one of the "facts" is that you have to ship products to your customer only on Tuesday morning. But if you challenge that assumption ("fact") you might discover that the customer would be just as satisfied with shipments on Tuesday evening or Wednesday morning, which could simplify your delivery person's schedule.
    - *Mental models.* Many times we hold to faulty assumptions about why we were assigned a project or given a certain goal or assignment; these faulty assumptions have a powerful effect on our emotions and our behavior at work. For example, if you had an assumption at work that says, "There's no way this problem can be solved, I don't know why they gave it to me; someone must really have it in for me," what kind of behavior would that lead to? It would probably lead to feelings of frustration, skepticism, cynicism, anger, and resentment; and it would also probably not prompt you to give it your best effort, reasoning "It can't be done anyway, so why should I kill myself trying?" It can be very helpful to challenge our mental models; when we bring them out into the open we can then see them for what they are (beliefs, not facts written in stone) and we are then empowered to change them into more constructive mental models that allow us to learn from our day-to-day experiences. Try this exercise:
        - Think about your hidden assumptions (mental models) about an upcoming or current experience.
        - List some of those assumptions in your Learning Journal.

- For each assumption, list 2-3 questions that you can ask yourself or your direct manager to gain more detailed information that will help you validate or invalidate the assumption.
- When you have answered the questions about the assumptions, identify a new mental model or models that better equips you to both successfully execute the assignment as well as learn, grow, and develop while doing so.

- *Learning goals.* One very practical way to reframe your experience as a learning opportunity is to create a goal around something you want to learn from engaging in the experience.
  - Think about the experience and identify areas, domains, or topics that you know a lot about, and areas that you know less about.
  - Choose 1 or 2 areas that you believe would be valuable for you to know more about, and establish a goal to learn something about it.
  - Establish a schedule to monitor your progress against this learning goal, just as you would a business goal or objective.
  - Revisit progress against the goal, and revise it or set a new goal when you are read.

- *Learning questions.* Another practical way to reframe your experience as a learning opportunity is to ask "learning questions" about the assignment and situation. Learning questions require you to suspend your judgment about the situation and to proactively explore it to help gain a deeper understanding.
  - One way to do this is to use the old "tried and true" Who, What, When, Where, and How questions
    - **Who** will be involved in this assignment/experience? What do I know about them and their background, capabilities, or network of relationships in the company and industry? What can I learn from them? Who are the key stakeholders for the assignment/experience? What would be a "win"

for each of them? Who are the resisters or skeptics that you will need to influence or win over, in order to successfully accomplish the assignment?

  - Who has been through an assignment/experience like this before, and what did they learn?
  - Who could act as your mentor or learning partner during this experience?

- **What** is the assignment/experience about on the surface? What is the stated objective or deliverable? What does success look like? What is the context within which this assignment is taking place? What led up to the current situation that you don't know about yet? What has been done previously in relation to this assignment?

  - What are my assumptions about the assignment? How can I challenge these assumptions and look at the assignment/opportunity differently, e.g., more positively?
  - What knowledge, skills, and competencies do you need or want to develop by engaging in this experience? What are your learning goals or objectives?

- **When** is the deliverable or objective due to be accomplished? When did the company last attempt to address the issue that this assignment is focused on? Is the time frame realistic, or do you need to renegotiate either the due date or the deliverable? Are there other time-related issues or questions, such as can the assignment be accomplished given the company's business cycle and other streams of work already underway or planned?

  - When will you set aside time for reflection, to ensure you learn from the experience?
  - When will you step back to evaluate your learning and developmental progress during the experience?

- **Where** will the assignment take place? Have you worked in that location before, or is it new to you? Does it involve relocating to another country? What will you need to do to be ready for the difference in cultures, languages, customs, etc.?
    - What do you think you will learn the most about in relation to working across the boundaries of culture, country, language, customs, and organizational culture?
- **How** will you prepare for the assignment/opportunity? If this is an international or global assignment that involves relocation, have you developed a Transition Plan to ensure you cover all the important bases, get to know the right people, begin to build your network, etc.? What information do you need to prepare?
    - How will you learn and develop the knowledge, skills, and competencies you need, through this experience?
    - How will you know that you are learning what you need to learn from the experience?

LOOK FOR WAYS TO LEARN SOMETHING NEW WHILE PURSUING YOUR WORK GOALS, ASSIGNMENTS, AND PROJECTS:

- Don't wait for your direct manager or Human Resources to come to you with a developmental opportunity. Go to them and make it known that you want more development.

- Participate in a Peer or Team Coaching group. Peer coaching brings together a small, diverse group of 4 – 8 committed colleagues to focus on real problems, challenges, or tasks. Using a flexible, but structured, process of reflective questioning and listening, and guided by an Action Learning coach, group members address organizational and individual leadership challenges, and as a result enhance their leadership capabilities. (For expert assistance on Peer, Team, and Group Coaching contact Aspire Consulting: steve@aspireconsulting.net). Peer Coaching emphasizes commitment and accountability for learning and action.

- Start or join a "True North" group. These groups provide a powerful avenue for taking responsibility for your own learning and development.

PERSISTENTLY WORK THROUGH DIFFICULT ISSUES AND OVERCOME OBSTACLES TO ACCOMPLISH DESIRED CHANGES:

- Another important aspect of taking responsibility for your own learning and development is how you handle obstacles or barriers to development. One of the reasons (excuses) leaders frequently give for not participating in development activities is that they "don't have enough time." Others object that the training is not relevant to their job, that they liked the training but no one else is using the new knowledge/skills in their department, that their boss should attend the training and change his/her behavior first, etc. The list of issues and obstacles is seemingly endless. The key here is to remember: you are not responsible for anyone else except you. If you are responsible for your own learning and development, then it is up to you to work through the issues and obstacles you encounter (and you will encounter them) in order to accomplish the changes you desire.

- Learning and development involve personal change, and it takes time to bring about significant, lasting change. Be realistic about how long it will take to accomplish your desired learning goals and objectives. Many times leaders are in a hurry to reach the next level, but are not willing to invest the effort and time it takes to get there. Make sure you don't have a "check the box" mentality, where just because you took a certain step or completed a specific assignment you believe that you have now "arrived" at your developmental destination. Persistence requires patience and reflection. Exercise both of those skills consistently, don't take your eyes off of the prize, and don't settle for the quick fix. Taking responsibility for your own learning and development also involves persistently working through difficult issues and overcoming obstacles to achieve your development goals.

Three Ways to Increase the Odds You'll Learn What You Set Out to Learn.

- Annie Murphy Paul, in Time magazine online (http://ideas.time.com/2013/03/25/how-to-increase-your-stamina-to-learn/) discusses three ways to increase the odds that you'll learn what you set out to learn, and not let obstacles stop you:

  o **Bring People With You**
    Why do you think most college students go to class? To see their friends. By contrast, much of the learning we do as adults — whether it's with an online course or a how-to manual or a video tutorial — we do on our own, accountable to no one. This makes it all too easy to quit. Some online courses are beginning to incorporate social media into their design, but connections forged this way are likely to be weak, especially at first. Better to recruit people you already know, whose opinions you care about, to sign up for that course or commit to a series of lessons along with you.

  o **Use Data to Motivate Yourself**
    Maybe you've heard about the Quantified Self movement — the oddly addictive practice of tracking every calorie consumed or burned, every minute spent online or asleep. This practice of using data to monitor and motivate yourself can be applied to learning endeavors too. Often, we get discouraged in our attempts to educate ourselves because we can't see the progress we're making. Keeping a record of your learning helps make that forward motion visible. It's important to put numbers to your efforts — hours practiced, problems completed, pages read — and it can be helpful to represent those numbers visually, in a graph or chart.

  o **Redesign Your 'Choice Architecture'**
    In their terrific book *Nudge*, authors Richard Thaler and Cass Sunstein note that "small and apparently insignificant details can have major impacts on people's behavior." Often,

it's not an insurmountable obstacle preventing us from pursuing learning, but rather a few minor hurdles that we never get around to addressing. *Now* is the time to print out that application, to schedule that first session with a coach. Sometimes getting over the initial hump is all you need.

- Or maybe you're actually good at getting started, and it's the middle and end stages where you bog down. As Thaler and Sunstein remark, "Never underestimate the power of inertia." But, they add, "that power can be harnessed" — harnessed to achieve your learning goals. This means making learning the default and *not* learning the more effortful or expensive option. Work with a music teacher who charges you for the lesson whether you show up or not (if you've paid for it, you will). Schedule a meeting to demonstrate your new skill to your colleagues (it's easier to learn it than to back out). "Choice architecture" is what Thaler and Sunstein call the context in which we make decisions. Make sure that the structures you build support learning — in the short term, and over the long haul."

The Power of "Grit"

- Persistence is a powerful force when it comes to working through difficult issues, overcoming obstacles, and learning. Heidi Grant Halvorson calls persistence "grit," a willingness to commit to long-term goals, and to persist in the face of difficulty.

  "Studies show that gritty people obtain more education in their lifetime, and earn higher college GPAs. Grit predicts which cadets will stick out their first grueling year at West Point. In fact, grit even predicts which round contestants will make it to at the Scripps National Spelling Bee."

  The good news is, if you aren't particularly gritty now, there is something you can do about it. People who lack grit more often than not believe that they just don't have the innate abilities successful people have. If that describes your own thinking . . . well, there's no way to put this nicely: you are wrong. As I mentioned earlier, effort, planning, persistence, and good strategies are what it really takes to succeed. Embracing this knowledge will not only help you see yourself and your goals more accurately, but also do wonders for your grit."

- **Persistence over the long haul** was ranked as *the #1 most powerful strategy for setting and achieving challenging goals* in research into "Nine Things Successful People Do Differently" conducted by Heidi Grant Halvorson and published in an HBR Blog. (See the full list at the end of this section.) She commented on this finding:

  - "I wonder how many people have ever thought to blame their own failures on "not hanging in there long enough?" In my experience, very few. Instead we assume we lack the ability to succeed. We decide that we don't have what it takes – whatever that is – to meet the challenge. And we really couldn't be more wrong. *Grit is not an innate gift. Persisting is something we learn to do, when (and if) we realize how well it pays off.*

  - Or take "knowing how far you have left to go" (the #2 most impactful strategy) … Even someone with a healthy amount of grit (persistence) will probably find his or her motivation flagging if they don't have a clear sense of where they are now and where they want to end up. How much weight would a contestant on The Biggest Loser lose if he only weighed himself at the beginning and the end, instead of once a week? How well would an Olympic-level athlete perform is she only timed her official races, and never her practices? We can see how essential monitoring is for others' performance, and yet somehow miss its importance for our own.

  - Does that mean that the items further down the list aren't as important? Not quite. For instance, #7, "focusing on getting better, rather than being good," actually predicted using each of the other eight things! People who focused on "being good," on the other hand, were less likely to use the other tactics on the list. In fact, if you do a lot of "be good" thinking, you are less likely to be gritty or have willpower, and you are more likely to tempt fate. You're also, not surprisingly, less likely to reach your goals."

Nine Things Successful People Do Differently

- **Have Grit** – Persistence over the long haul is key

- **Know Exactly How Far You Have Left to Go** – Monitor your progress

- **Get Specific** – Have a crystal-clear idea of exactly what success will look like

- **Seize the Moment to Act on Your Goals** – Know in advance what you will do, and when and where you will do it

- **Focus on What You Will Do, Not What You Won't Do** – Instead of focusing on bad habits, it's more effective to replace them with better ones

- **Build Your Willpower Muscle** – If you don't have enough willpower, you can get more using it

- **Focus on Getting Better, Rather Than Being Good** – Think about your goals as opportunities to improve, rather than to prove yourself

- **Be a Realistic Optimist** – Visualize how you will make success happen by overcoming obstacles

- **Don't Tempt Fate** – No one has willpower all the time, so don't push your luck

  - From Heidi Grant Halvorson, http://blogs.hbr.org/2011/02/nine-things-successful-people/ and (http://blogs.hbr.org/2013/03/the-most-effective-strategies/)

"I learned very early in my career that I needed to take full responsibility for my own learning and development. There were times when I had access to company issued programs but even then, I maximized my learning by putting complete focus and commitment on the program, follow-up and on-the-job application (where the best learning takes place)."

Exemplary Learning Leader

Self-Assessment: Score Yourself on Taking Responsibility for Your Own Learning and Development

Think about your work and life experiences over the past year and answer the following questions using this scale:

Never (1)	Rarely (2)	Sometimes (3)	Often (4)	Almost always (5)

- I feel personally accountable to actively pursue my own professional growth and development   1   2   3   4   5

- I take the initiative to improve my leadership capabilities   1   2   3   4   5

- I develop goals and action plans to improve my knowledge and/or abilities related to my job or career   1   2   3   4   5

- I intentionally reframe my experiences to view them as learning opportunities   1   2   3   4   5

- I look for ways to learn something new while pursuing my work goals, assignments, and projects   1   2   3   4   5

- I persistently work through difficult issues and overcome obstacles to accomplish desired changes   1   2   3   4   5

OVERALL SCORE:
Sum of Ratings divided by 6 (Number of Items)

Guide to Interpreting Your Overall Score

- If your overall score on this learning practice is 18 or less, it's time to actively take greater individual responsibility for your learning and development, rather than letting experiences go unmined for learning, or waiting for learning opportunities to be offered by your employer and/or Leadership Development department. Refer to the Potential Recommended Actions for ideas on how you can more effectively take responsibility for your development as a leader.

- If your overall score on this learning practice is 19 to 23, you are already taking responsibility to some degree but could still be more proactive as the "owner" of your own development. Explore the Potential Recommended Actions for possible ways you can exhibit more individual responsibility for your leadership development through experience.

- If your overall score on this learning practice is 24 or above, congratulations! You are taking personal responsibility for your learning and development. Keep it up and continue to be the primary owner of your growth as a leader!

REFLECTION QUESTIONS

What VUCA challenges does your organization face?

How important is it to your organization that leaders have the mindset and skills needed to address those VUCA challenges?

What are three concrete examples you taking responsibility for your own learning, growth, and development as a leader?

What is one concrete example of you _not_ taking personal responsibility for your own learning, growth, and development as a leader? What were the consequences?

Describe a situation in which you took the initiative to improve your leadership capabilities without the support or encouragement of your organization.

Think of a work challenge/assignment you face today. What is your plan to learn something new while pursuing this challenge/assignment?

2. Approach New Assignments/Opportunities with Openness to Experience and Positive Intention to Learn

"You have to be open minded and flexible to make sure you can influence people and work with them to get the results that you are looking for, and that role might be a straight highway in some places, and other places you might have to go up the hills and down the valley and up the hills to get what you want."

Lou – Brazilian corporate leader

Introduction

Approaching new assignments and opportunities with openness to experience and a positive intention to learn is essential to maximizing your learning from experience. This learning practice is in essence active preparation for learning, in which you adopt or enact an attitude of positive expectation and openness to learn from situations before you experience them. Negative attitudes or expectations limit performance, drain motivation, and inhibit learning, while positive attitudes or expectations typically boost performance, enhance motivation, and incite learning.

Review the list of behaviors, behavioral trends and patterns, and tendencies below. As you do, reflect on your own experience and try to recall specific situations or events that shed light on your own patterns of behavior related to this Learning Practice.

BEHAVIORS, BEHAVIORAL TRENDS AND PATTERNS, TENDENCIES:

- Automatically think to yourself when you have a new assignment, "This is a great opportunity to learn something new"
- Welcome assignments to projects or tasks that you have never done before
- Look forward to different types of experiences because of the learning you might gain
- Find something useful to learn in most experiences
- Intentionally look for something to learn, even when an experience is difficult, challenging, or not to your liking

Potential Developmental Actions

Review the following for examples of developmental actions you can take to enhance your effectiveness at approaching new assignments / opportunities with openness to experience and positive intention to learn. Identify at least one or two actions that you will work to integrate into your day-to-day work life.

AUTOMATICALLY THINK TO YOURSELF WHEN YOU HAVE A NEW ASSIGNMENT, "THIS IS A GREAT OPPORTUNITY TO LEARN SOMETHING NEW"

- Managing your reactions to new assignments and experiences is an important aspect of learning from experience. To some degree, you need to recognize that, although you may not be able to control the circumstances of your work life, you do have control over how you respond to those circumstances. When you are given a new assignment, check your initial reaction to the assignment. Are you reacting positively or negatively? Try to identify why you are reacting the way you are reacting. If you are reacting negatively, try making a list of the pros and cons of the assignment, and then focus on the pros.

- Focus on your inner "self-talk," the dialogue you have with yourself when contemplating your work life. In The Brilliant Blog by Annie Murphy Paul, self-talk is described as a key tool to help us manage ourselves when learning.

    - "In the privacy of our minds, we all talk to ourselves – an inner monologue that might seem rather pointless. As one scientific paper on self-talk asks: "What can we tell ourselves that we don't already know?" But as that study and others go on to show, the act of giving ourselves mental messages can help us learn and perform at our best. Researchers have identified the most effective forms of self-talk, collected here – so that the next time you talk to yourself, you know exactly what you should say.

    - Self-talk isn't just motivation messages like "You can do it!" or "Almost there," although this internal cheering section can give us confidence. A review of more than two dozen studies, published in 2011 in the journal Perspectives on Psychological Science, found that there's another kind of mental message that is even more useful, called "instructional self-talk." This is the kind of running commentary we engage in when we're carrying out a difficult task, especially one that's unfamiliar to us. Think about when you were first learning how to drive. Your self-talk might have gone something like this: "Foot on the gas pedal, hands on the wheel, slow down for the curve here, now put your blinker on…"

- o Over time, of course, giving yourself instructions becomes unnecessary – but while you're learning, it does three important things. First, it **enhances our attention**, focusing us on the important elements of the task and screen out distractions. Second, it helps us **regulate our effort** and make decisions about what to do, how to do it, and when. And third, self-talk allows us to **control our cognitive and emotional reactions**, steadying us so we stay on task.

- o In a recent study of students learning to throw darts in a gym class, Athanasios Kolovelonis and his colleagues at the University of Thessaly in Greece found that self-talk is most effective when incorporated into a cycle of thought and action. First comes forethought, when you **set a goal** for yourself and make a plan for how to get there. That's followed by **performance**, when you enact the plan to the best of your ability. Last comes **self-reflection**, when you carefully evaluate what you've done and adjust your plan for the next time.

- o Self-talk can play a key part in this cycle. During the forethought phase, consider carefully what you'll say to yourself. You can even write out a script. Repeat these self-instructions during the performance phase. With practice, you may find that your self-instructions become abbreviated; research has found that the so-called "cue words" can become powerful signals. In a study of elite sprinters, for example, the runners spoke certain words to themselves at certain times: "push" during the acceleration phase of the sprint, "heel" during the maximum-speed phase, and "claw" during the endurance phase. When they used these cue words, the athletes ran faster.

- o After the action is over, consider how you might change your self-talk to improve your performance next time – so that at the moment it matters, the right words are ringing in your ears."

    - Annie Murphy Paul, The Brilliant Blog. http://anniemurphypaul.com/2013/12/the-right-way-to-talk-to-yourself/

- Reflect on your reaction to your next new assignment, and try to look at yourself from a distance, as if you were a third party observing who had the ability to know your thoughts and feelings. What are you thinking and feeling about the new assignment?

    - o If your thoughts and feelings are based on a prior experience that was negative, acknowledge that, set those thoughts and feelings aside, and then think about your new assignment with a fresh, unbiased perspective. Don't let previous negative experiences prevent you from seeing the positive in the present opportunities.

- Share your reactions to your next new assignment with a trusted colleague or friend, and ask them how they see things. Sometimes just the act of saying your thoughts, reactions, or concerns out loud will help clarify or bring things into perspective.
    - When you talk with your colleague or friend, be sure to intentionally maintain an open mind and listen closely to what they say.
    - Listen for positive aspects of the new assignment, and write them down. Creating a written record or list of the positive aspects can help bring balance to your perspective, and it will remind you of the possibilities for learning, growth, and development inherent in the situation.

WELCOME ASSIGNMENTS TO PROJECTS OR TASKS THAT YOU HAVE NEVER DONE BEFORE

- When beginning a new assignment, always ask yourself, "What can I learn from this?"
- How do you typically react to a new assignment, project, or task that you have never done before? Do you welcome it or do you react with fear? There are many reasons we react with fear to new assignments, projects, and tasks. If you react with fear or another "negative" emotion/feeling, try to understand what is driving that reaction. Make a list of all the reasons that you are reacting the way you are reacting to the assignment. Now see if you can find the positive aspects of the assignment; try to identify at least as many reasons to feel positive about it as negative about it.
- Fear and anxiety about change and new, different situations is understandable. If you react to new assignments with fear and anxiety instead of welcoming such assignments, one way of reducing that fear and anxiety is to gather as much information about the assignment as you can. Much of this type of reaction is based on a lack of solid information about what the assignment holds for you: Who will I be working with? What will be expected or required of me? Am I up to the challenge? Will I find this to be rewarding? Do I have to do this assignment and maintain my current responsibilities at the same time? To deal with your emotional reaction,

make a list of all the questions you can think of that you're wondering about. Then, organize them into logical categories. Next, figure out how you can get answers to your questions. Now go about getting your questions answered, and as you do pay attention to your emotional state. You will probably find that, with more information you begin to feel a bit less anxious, and more able to cope with the unknown, because you will know more. However, be aware that other questions may surface based on the information you discover, so just add those questions to the updated list and continue seeking information. Over time, as you gather information your emotional state will evolve and change as your questions get answered. Some questions may not have answers; and you may not like the answers to some questions. But you will have a more fact-based foundation from which to move forward into the new assignment/situation.

LOOK FORWARD TO DIFFERENT TYPES OF EXPERIENCES BECAUSE OF THE LEARNING YOU MIGHT GAIN

- If you find that you do not automatically look at a new assignment as an opportunity to learn, try to understand what is leading to your reaction to the assignment, and remind yourself that you have an opportunity ahead.

- If you find yourself feeling hesitant about a new project or task, take the time to reflect deeply about the assignment. What about it causes your hesitation? What can you do to reduce the hesitation or concern, so you can begin to feel more positive and optimistic about it?

- Make a list of the tasks, activities, challenges, and problems you might encounter in an upcoming, unfamiliar experience. What you can learn from each item on the list? How can learning that be a benefit to you in your growth and development as a leader? What is at least one aspect of the experience that is interesting to you? Write down a statement describing what you are looking forward to in the upcoming experience, and why you are looking forward to it.

FIND SOMETHING USEFUL TO LEARN IN MOST EXPERIENCES

- When beginning a new assignment, always ask yourself, "What can I learn from this?"

- Throughout a new experience, continually remind yourself to be open to new things.

- Take time at the end of the day to reflect on what you learned, to identify unexpected successes and failures, and think about any patterns that emerge in how you are leading.

- Keep a log of what you learn from significant work experiences. Periodically review your "learning log" to see what you have learned from which experience. What themes or trends do you see? Do you see the same items over and over? Do you need to do something differently in order to get past a "learning plateau," where you seem to be going over and over the same learning? How have you applied the learning to your work as a leader? How can you apply the learning to your work as a leader?

INTENTIONALLY LOOK FOR SOMETHING TO LEARN, EVEN WHEN AN EXPERIENCE IS DIFFICULT, CHALLENGING, OR NOT TO YOUR LIKING

- When given an assignment or task you have never done before, immediately begin looking for what you might learn from it. Break it down into the various elements that you are more and less familiar with, comfortable with, or know more or less about. Find something in the assignment or project that you can learn about, and make it your goal to become an expert on that topic or area.

- If you continue to have concerns about an assignment or find it to be difficult, challenging, or not to your liking, focus more on what you can learn instead of how hard it is.

- Build reflection into your work; ask yourself "How open am I being to the new experiences I am encountering?" Also ask yourself "What do I intend to learn?" from each experience you encounter or are engaged in.

- When an experience is difficult or challenging, remind yourself that it seems that way because you don't understand something about it, or you don't yet have the mindset, capabilities, or skills to deal with it successfully. Take it on as an opportunity to learn. Sometimes you have to learn something unexpected before you can successfully solve a problem or achieve a goal. This is especially true when you are encountering different cultures. Make it your goal to intentionally look for something to learn whenever you encounter unexpected, or expected, difficulties, challenges, problems, or resistance.

- When an assignment is not to your liking, you are at risk of not giving it your best effort. However, it may present one of your best learning and development opportunities, because assignments and experiences that go against our preferred ways of thinking and acting give us the chance to try out unfamiliar approaches. These kinds of assignments will take you out of your comfort zone, and as a result...you will be uncomfortable. Accept that discomfort as the price of growth, and make it your mission to learn something valuable from the experience.

Listening and Observing with Intention

Listening and observing can be passive activities – in one ear and out the other, as mom used to say. Or they can be rich, active, intense experiences that lead to serious learning. The difference lies in our intention: the purpose and awareness with which we approach the situation.

Listening with Intention

- o "Skilled listeners go into a listening session with a sense of what they want to get out of it. They set a goal for their listening, and they generate predictions about what the speaker will say. Before the talking begins, they mentally review what they already know about the subject, and form an intention to "listen out for" what's important or relevant." (Annie Murphy Paul, The Brilliant Blog, http://anniemurphypaul.com/2013/10/the-power-of-intention/)

- o When listening, these learners maintain their focus and bring it back to the words being spoken if their attention wanders. They don't get distracted by confusing details, but instead take notes of what they don't understand and try to make inferences about what those things might mean, based on their previous knowledge, the context of the talk, the identity of the speaker, etc. They "listen for gist" and don't get too caught up in the fine details. All the while, they evaluate what they're hearing and their own understanding of it. They check their inferences to see if they're correct and identify the questions they still have so they can pursue the answers later.

- o Research shows that learners who use these listening skills are better at processing and storing new information, better at finding the best ways to practice, and better at reinforcing what they have learned.

Observing with Intention

- o Once again, and all together now: we learn by doing. But we also can learn a lot by watching, or observing. We learn to dance the salsa first by watching the teacher run through a sequence of steps and moves, then practicing the salsa ourselves; we learn tennis first by watching a coach demonstrate proper serving technique, then practicing serving ourselves; we learn science by watching a science professor conducting a dissection, then practicing dissection ourselves. Observing experts, combined with application and practice, is a great way to hone our own skills.

- o "This is especially true in the case of motor movements, and research in neuroscience is beginning to show why: when we watch someone else's motions, the parts of the brain that direct our own physical movements are activated. Observation accelerates the learning process because our brains are able to map others' actions onto our own mental representations, making them more detailed and more accurate . . . We derive the most benefit from observation when we have in mind the conscious intention to carry out the action ourselves." (Annie Murphy Paul, The Brilliant Blog, http://anniemurphypaul.com/2013/10/the-power-of-intention/)

- o Observing is much more than simply, passively "watching" someone else do something. Observing requires attention, focus, and purposefully soaking in everything you can about the person and action you are observing.

- o If you don't have a goal to learn something specific from a new experience or assignment, turn all your "antennae" on so you can capture everything that is going on, and intentionally look for something new to learn. This kind of "mindful awareness" requires that you intentionally take down your barriers as you feel your way through the experience. As you maintain this high level of openness and intentionality, you will need to periodically reflect and process the events in order to draw meaning and learning from them.

Self-Assessment: Score Yourself on Approaching New Assignments / Opportunities with Openness to Experience and Positive Intention to Learn

Think about your work and life experiences over the past year and answer the following questions using this scale:

Never (1)   Rarely (2)   Sometimes (3)   Often (4)   Almost always (5)

- I automatically think to myself when I have a new assignment, "This is a great opportunity to learn something new."   1   2   3   4   5

- I welcome assignments to projects or tasks that I have never done before.   1   2   3   4   5

- I look forward to different types of experiences because of the learning I might gain.   1   2   3   4   5

- I find something useful to learn in most experiences.   1   2   3   4   5

- I intentionally look for something to learn, even when an experience is difficult, challenging, or not to my liking.   1   2   3   4   5

OVERALL SCORE:
Sum of Ratings divided by 5 (Number of Items)

Guide to Interpreting Your Overall Score

- If your overall score on this learning practice is 15 or less, it's time to rethink how you approach new assignments/opportunities. How can you be more open to these experiences? What can you do to take on a more positive attitude about them? Refer to the Potential Developmental Actions for ideas on how you can more effectively integrate this Learning Practice into your work life.

- If your overall score on this learning practice is 16 to 20, you are already approaching experiences with openness to learning. How can you become even more open to experience? What can you do to intentionally adopt a positive attitude focused on learning from your assignments? Review the Potential Developmental Actions for ideas on how you can more effectively engage in new assignments/opportunities.

- If your overall score on this learning practice is 21 or above, congratulations! You are actively engaged in maximizing your learning and development. Keep it up and continue to be open to experience and look for learning in every experience!

REFLECTION QUESTIONS

What new assignments or opportunities have you encountered during the past year?

To what degree did you approach those assignments/opportunities with a positive attitude, openness to the experiences, and a positive intention to learn from them?

Describe specifically what you did that illustrates how you were open to the experiences.

What is one concrete example of you taking on a new assignment solely or primarily with the purpose of learning something new?

Describe an experience you had that was difficult, challenging, or not to your liking. What did you do to intentionally look for something to learn?

How have you coached or mentored others to approach new challenges and assignments as learning opportunities, and to exhibit openness to the experience?

Describe a situation when you were unable to learn something valuable from an assignment or opportunity. What was the assignment? How did you try to learn from it? What prevented you from learning from that experience? What would you do differently if you could do it again?

3. Seek and Use Feedback

"When I think about being a great global leader, it's almost like you have to find your soul, and you have to know what really makes you tick, and then you have to believe in it, and you have to go for it, and then you just have to make sure that when you do fail, take it as a gift. Or when you get feedback, instead of being defensive, take it as a gift and learn and grow from it, because it ends up being incredibly rewarding."

Senior HR Leader in a Global Consumer Products Company

Introduction

Feedback is sometimes associated with criticism or other negative information that is unhelpfully dumped on someone in the mistaken belief that it will inspire or motivate that individual to change, perform better, or improve in some way. The mistaken belief that feedback is "negative" can cause us to avoid seeking and receiving constructive feedback that could be very helpful to our growth and development. To the contrary, when a leader actively seeks out, listens to, and uses feedback, it can be an accelerator of growth. As it's said: "Feedback is a gift!"

Review the list of behaviors, behavioral trends and patterns, and tendencies below. As you do, reflect on your own experience and try to recall specific situations or events that shed light on your own patterns of behavior related to this Learning Practice.

BEHAVIORS, BEHAVIORAL TRENDS AND PATTERNS, TENDENCIES:

- Ask colleagues (such as your direct manager/supervisor, peers, customers, stakeholders, and/or direct reports) for feedback about your performance, behaviors and/or competencies
- Listen closely to feedback you receive
- Listen closely to what might NOT be said (behind the words)
- Follow up with and thank your colleagues for giving you useful feedback
- Take feedback, both positive and constructive, to heart, and do your best to use it to change, grow, and develop

Potential Developmental Actions

Review the following for examples of developmental actions you can take to enhance your effectiveness seeking and using feedback for development. Identify at least one or two actions that you will work to integrate into your day-to-day work life.

ASK COLLEAGUES (SUCH AS YOUR DIRECT MANAGER/SUPERVISOR, PEERS, CUSTOMERS, STAKEHOLDERS, AND/OR DIRECT REPORTS) FOR FEEDBACK ABOUT YOUR PERFORMANCE AND/OR COMPETENCIES:

- To get started with seeking feedback, start small but take a small risk at the same time: approach someone you trust and who knows you well and ask them for feedback about a specific aspect of your performance.

- Make sure you ask someone who knows something about your performance so you will be more likely to receive valuable input. For example, your peers are likely to provide more meaningful feedback about your ability to collaborate and work as a team member, while your direct reports may provide better feedback about your communication, coaching, and giving feedback and direction. Your direct supervisor may have a more informed perspective about your ability to think strategically, plan, and how you handle challenges.

- Try to get feedback from various sources, not just one or two people who are your friends and allies. When you solicit feedback from people who don't necessarily share your worldview or perspective on life, you have the opportunity to gain valuable insights that you would not otherwise have.

- Marshall Goldsmith, an expert in executive development, feedback, and coaching has developed a widely used approach to encouraging and using feedback[7]. The steps in his recommended feedback process are:
  - **Ask** - Peter Drucker said that in organizations of the past, the role of the leader was to tell. In organizations today and of the future, the role of the leader is to ask. This is easy to say and difficult to do. It takes courage. Ask your peers and employees, customers and

---

[7] "Leadership is a Contact Sport." Marshall Goldsmith, http://www.marshallgoldsmith.com/articles/leadership-is-a-contact-sport-an-8-step-leadership-development-model-for-success/

suppliers, "How am I doing?" People need to feel that it is safe to be honest - that there will be no reprisals for their candidness. Choose an appropriate time and place to ask for feedback. Research tells us that people tend not to give candid personal feedback in a group situation.

- **Listen** - Listen to what people are telling you. Attempt to listen without judging what the person is saying. Listen without expressing your opinion or responding. Inquire further to ascertain that you have an accurate view of what the person shared. Consider taking notes - writing down what the person says will help you reflect on the information later on.

- **Think** - Before you respond be aware of your reaction - the thoughts you've begun forming. Most of us want to jump right in with our rationalizations, excuses, perspectives, or ideas. Consider and reflect upon the person's perceptions of your leadership behavior. Work on developing your understanding of how others perceive your behavior and its impact – the intended and the unintended consequences on that person, other employees, and the work environment.

- **Thank** - This is a vitally important and often overlooked step in the feedback process. It's critical to thank people for taking the time and giving their effort to provide you with feedback. Thanking people helps to validate their efforts and demonstrates your seriousness to the process.

- **Respond** - There are three guidelines for responding to feedback:
  - Keep it positive
  - Keep it simple
  - Keep it focused

- **Involve** - Involve a wide circle of colleagues, employees, partners, and customers in this process. The key to involvement is mutual respect.

- **Change** - People can and do change. Choose one or two behaviors to focus on in developing your action plan. Identify concrete, observable actions to do differently. Monitor how well you are doing by keeping track of what you committed to change.

- **Follow-up** - This step is the most critical one. Follow-up demonstrates that you are truly committed to changing your behavior. Marshall suggests that you say to people, "You know that I am working on being a better listener. How am I doing? If you had any suggestions for me, what would they be?"

LISTEN CLOSELY TO THE FEEDBACK YOU RECEIVE ABOUT YOUR PERFORMANCE AND/OR COMPETENCIES &
LISTEN CLOSELY TO WHAT MIGHT NOT BE SAID (BEHIND THE WORDS):

- When someone is giving you feedback, keep your attention focused on that person and what they are saying to you. Resist becoming distracted or reacting emotionally to either the message or the tone of their message. This is where Learning Practice #6, Listen Transformatively, becomes important: listen intently, deeply, empathically.

- Write down what you heard! It's much too easy to forget what someone told us, because of the busy schedules we have and lives we lead. And even easier if we don't like what they said. After a few hours, days, or weeks, a piece of meaningful feedback can be lost to a fading memory.

- If what you hear upsets you, remember to breathe. Breathe again. Slowly. Do nothing but breathe for 15 seconds, while you let emotion and tension fade away. Then, count to 10. Reflect on what they said, and if necessary, clarify by repeating or paraphrasing what you heard them say back to them, and ask "Is that what you mean?"

    - If you need to "listen between the lines" – infer what they mean because you don't understand from their words directly – take your time and try to restate what you think you heard them say, and ask "Did I get that right?"

    - Probe deeper, beyond the exact words they use. Sometimes people couch messages in polite language so that you won't be offended, hoping that you'll understand what they're trying to tell you and that you won't be upset. This can be very valuable information, so listen! Ask clarifying questions to make sure you really understand, and remember… Breathe. Count to 10. Breathe again. Then respond…

- When you ask for feedback, you open yourself up to surprises, to hearing something you didn't anticipate, or learning something that is upsetting. When this happens, look at it as a chance to practice your emotional intelligence skills, especially self-awareness and self-management, the two key skills that enable you to have social awareness and to effectively manage relationships.

FOLLOW UP WITH AND THANK YOUR COLLEAGUES FOR GIVING YOU USEFUL FEEDBACK ABOUT YOUR PERFORMANCE AND/OR COMPETENCIES:

- Remember to say "Thank you" to whoever gives you feedback. It can be just as difficult for the feedback giver as the feedback receiver! And also remember that they will be watching to see what – if anything – changes as a result of taking a risk and giving you feedback. If you do nothing, you risk damaging your relationship with that individual or reinforcing negative opinions and feelings about you.

The Impact of Feedback Follow-Up

- Keilty, Goldsmith & Co. (Marshall Goldsmith) designed a study to look at the impact of follow-up on leadership effectiveness. In this study co-workers of participants were asked:
    - Did this person become a more effective leader?
    - Did this person initially respond concerning her/his feedback?
    - How frequently did this person follow-up concerning her/his progress?
- The results follow:

o   **Table 1:** Leaders who were seen as not responding to feedback and not following-up were perceived as only slightly more effective than they had been 18 months earlier. While 48% were rated as more effective, more than half were rated as unchanged or less effective. This statistic is similar to what you would see by random chance - "the attendance award."

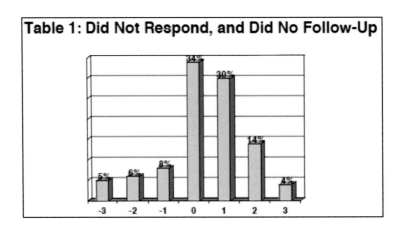

o   **Table 2:** Leaders who were seen as responding but doing no follow-up were perceived as no more effective than managers who did not respond at all. In fact, this group had the highest percentage of leaders who were perceived as getting worse. Raising expectations without producing results engenders dissatisfaction and decreased respect.

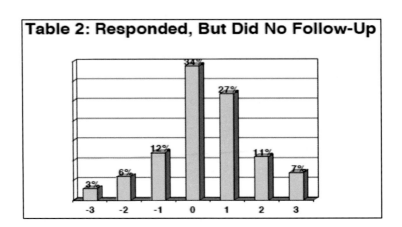

- **Table 3:** Even a little follow-up has a positive impact. Approximately two-thirds of the leaders in this group were viewed as more effective. One third were rated as unchanged or less effective.

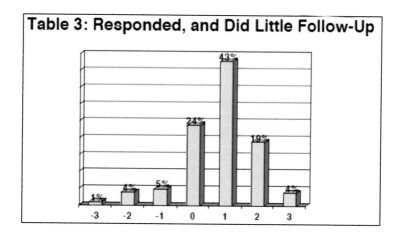

- **Table 4:** Leaders who did some follow-up experienced another positive shift in scores with 89% rated as more effective. Almost half of the leaders in this group were rated in the highest two categories and almost none were seen as less effective.

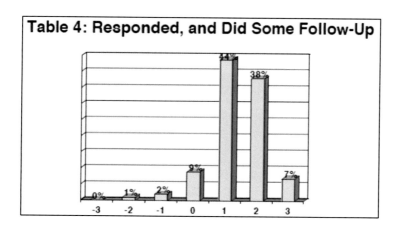

o **Table 5:** Leaders who engaged in frequent follow-up were almost invariably perceived as more effective. This group showed a major increase in the positive categories, as well as three times more leaders in the highest category.

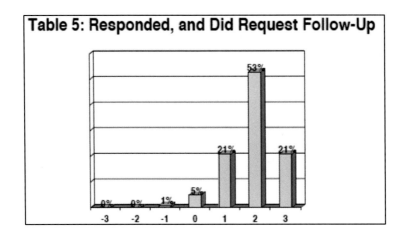

o **Table 6:** This table shows the dramatic positive impact of consistent or periodic follow-up. More than half of the leaders are rated in the highest possible category, while 86% are rated either +2 or +3.

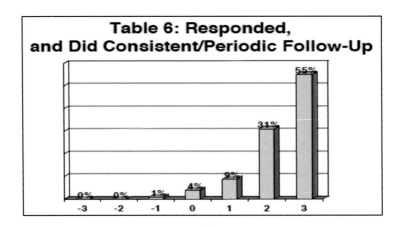

- Follow-up works! (Source: "Leadership is a Contact Sport." Marshall Goldsmith, 2002)

TAKE FEEDBACK, BOTH POSITIVE AND CONSTRUCTIVE, TO HEART, AND DO MY BEST TO USE IT TO CHANGE, GROW, AND DEVELOP:

- Reflect on the feedback: revisit or replay it in your mind, making certain you recall the key messages accurately and as the feedback give seemed to intend them.

- Consider whether or not you need to change your behavior or leadership style in response to the feedback. It may not be imperative to change, or to change radically. On the other hand, the feedback giver may expect you to change, or may require you to change. It's really up to you, but make sure you consider the consequences of not changing before taking that road. Most times, feedback really is a gift, and accepting it in that way means you have the option to accept it and do something with it, or not to respond.

- The hardest part of implementing this Learning Practice may be doing something about the feedback. If you decide to take action to change something about your behavior, performance, or development, consider telling that person what you plan to do, and ask them to help you by keeping an eye out for evidence that you are changing. Look for the next opportunity to take action, and be sure to circle back around to the people who gave you feedback to close the loop. A simple "How am I doing on _____?" is all that's needed.

- Share your decision to take action on feedback with a trusted colleague, friend, or family member. Their perspectives may be helpful in keeping you on track with your change goals. Ask them to help you by letting you know when they either see evidence of changed behavior or a recurrence of behavior that you are trying to change.

- Get out your calendar, or open Outlook, Google Calendar, or your usual way of organizing your time. During the 15 – 30 minutes you set aside for reflection every week, revisit the feedback and the change you are trying to bring about in yourself. Think about what actions you took during the previous week to address the feedback. Make a list of actions you plan to take during the coming week to improve in relation to the feedback.

- Go back to the people who gave you the feedback you asked for, and ask for a "check-up." Give it enough time and serious effort to make change visible, and then ask them again "How am I doing?" in relation to the feedback they gave and the change goal that you set.

Self-Assessment: Score Yourself on Seeking and Using Feedback

Think about your work and life experiences over the past year and answer the following questions using this scale:

Never (1)   Rarely (2)   Sometimes (3)   Often (4)   Almost always (5)

- I ask colleagues (such as my direct manager/supervisor, peers, customers, stakeholders, and/or direct reports) for feedback about my performance, behaviors, and/or competencies.   **1   2   3   4   5**

- I listen closely to feedback I receive.   **1   2   3   4   5**

- I listen closely to what might NOT be said (behind the words).   **1   2   3   4   5**

- I follow up with and thank my colleagues for giving me useful feedback.   **1   2   3   4   5**

- I take feedback, both positive and constructive, to heart, and do my best to use it to change, grow, and develop.   **1   2   3   4   5**

OVERALL SCORE:
Sum of Ratings divided by 5 (Number of Items)

Guide to Interpreting Your Overall Score

- If your overall score on this learning practice is 15 or less, it's time to explore the power of feedback as a development tool. How can you obtain more honest, useful feedback? How can you increase your use of feedback? Refer to the Potential Developmental Actions for ideas on how you can more effectively integrate this Learning Practice into your work life.

- If your overall score on this learning practice is 16 to 20, you are already using feedback as a means of growth and development. What can you do to obtain deeper, more meaningful feedback? How can you demonstrate your commitment to using feedback to change, grow, and develop? Review the Potential Developmental Actions for ideas on how you can enhance your use of feedback as a development tool.

- If your overall score on this learning practice is 21 or above, congratulations! You are actively engaged in leveraging feedback as a means of development. Keep it up and continue to look for feedback from a wide range of people who know you and your work!

REFLECTION QUESTIONS

Think back over the past year and reflect on how you have asked for feedback about yourself as a leader. Who did you ask for feedback? What did you ask them? What did you learn as a result?

How did you respond to the feedback that you received?

Describe a piece of challenging feedback you received in the past year. How did you take that feedback to heart and use it to grow, change, and develop?

How have you coached and mentored someone else to seek and use feedback for their own growth and development?

What have you done in the last year to improve your skill at giving and receiving feedback?

What is one thing you believe you could do to improve your effectiveness at seeking and using feedback to develop?

4. Develop a Clear Understanding of Your Strengths and Areas of Development

"There are three things extremely hard: steel, a diamond, and to know one's self."

Benjamin Franklin, 1750 Poor Richard's Almanac

Introduction

Developing a clear understanding of your strengths and areas of development is one of the most important steps you can take when pursuing development as a leader because it enables you to establish priorities for development. You may already have an idea of what you're good at and what you need to work on; many leaders do. The challenge we all face is that we are limited in our ability to accurately perceive ourselves, and so we have blind spots. Gaining additional information from a variety of sources, such as colleagues, peers, bosses, customers, etc. can be invaluable in terms of seeing ourselves realistically.

Review the list of behaviors, behavioral trends and patterns, and tendencies below. As you do, reflect on your own experience and try to recall specific situations or events that shed light on your own patterns of behavior related to this Learning Practice.

BEHAVIORS, BEHAVIORAL TRENDS AND PATTERNS, TENDENCIES:

- Take stock of your personality characteristics, and how they influence your performance and behavior at work
- Assess yourself against the leadership competencies in the competency model of your organization
- Ask others to help you by sharing their perspective on your strengths and areas for further development
- Identify your top strengths and top areas for further development

Potential Developmental Actions

Review the following for examples of developmental actions you can take to enhance your effectiveness at understanding your strengths and development needs as a leader. Identify at least one or two actions that you will work to integrate into your day-to-day work life.

TAKE STOCK OF YOUR PERSONALITY CHARACTERISTICS, AND HOW THEY INFLUENCE YOUR PERFORMANCE AND BEHAVIOR AT WORK:

- Complete a personality inventory to increase your self-awareness of your personality traits, characteristics, and behavior patterns that influence your performance and behavior at work
    - Work with a coach to gain access to an inventory or assessment tool, and to interpret the results
    - There are many different types of personality assessment instruments. Work with your coach to select one that best meets your needs and goals.
    - Take your time to understand the results of the inventory and the implications for you as a leader. Reflect on what the results reveal, and thoughtfully consider what they tell you about your strengths and areas of development. After you have distilled the results down to a few nuggets of insight that you believe are important, decide how you want to use these insights to enhance your development as a leader.

ASSESS YOURSELF AGAINST THE LEADERSHIP COMPETENCIES IN THE COMPETENCY MODEL OF YOUR ORGANIZATION:

- Complete a 360-degree leadership competency assessment, based on the leadership model of your organization.
- Work with your organization to organize and administer the 360-degree process. Many organizations have internal coaches who are able to interpret the results of these assessments.
- Take your time to understand the results of the 360-degree assessment and the implications for you as a leader. Reflect on what the results reveal, and thoughtfully consider what they tell you about your strengths and areas of development. After you have distilled the results down to a

few nuggets of insight that you believe are important, decide how you want to use these insights to enhance your development as a leader.

ASK OTHERS TO HELP YOU BY SHARING THEIR PERSPECTIVE ON YOUR STRENGTHS AND AREAS FOR FURTHER DEVELOPMENT:

- Nothing is quite as powerful as authentically asking for help from others. By becoming vulnerable and asking others to share their perspective on your strengths and areas for further development, you open yourself up to learning, build trust with others, and gain new insight into how others perceive you as a leader. In addition to the approach to asking for feedback discussed under Learning Practice #2, consider the following practical way of asking others for their help.

Try "FeedForward" Instead of Feedback

- Providing feedback has long been considered to be an essential skill for leaders. As they strive to achieve the goals of the organization, employees need to know how they are doing. They need to know if their performance is in line with what their leaders expect. They need to learn what they have done well and what they need to change. Traditionally, this information has been communicated in the form of "downward feedback" from leaders to their employees. Just as employees need feedback from leaders, leaders can benefit from feedback from their employees. Employees can provide useful input on the effectiveness of procedures and processes and as well as input to managers on their leadership effectiveness. This "upward feedback" has become increasingly common with the advent of 360° multi-rater assessments.
- But there is a fundamental problem with all types of feedback: it focuses on the past, on what has already occurred—not on the infinite variety of opportunities that can happen in the future. As such, feedback can be limited and static, as opposed to expansive and dynamic. So, if you have an aversion to feedback, you may be interested in an alternative!
- The following experiential exercise provides a powerful alternative to feedback. It can be conducted as part of a staff meeting, a training program, or a session devoted to leadership

development. In the exercise, each person plays two roles. In one role, they are asked provide feedforward – that is, to give someone else suggestions for the future and help as much as they can. In the second role, they are asked to accept feedforward—that is, to listen to the suggestions for the future and learn as much as they can. The exercise typically lasts for 10-15 minutes, and the average participant has 6-7 dialogue sessions. In the exercise, each person is asked to:

- o **Pick one behavior that you would like to change.** Change in this behavior should make a significant, positive difference in your life.
- o **Describe this behavior to a few randomly selected colleagues.** This is done in one-on-one dialogues. It can be done quite simply, such as, "I want to be a better listener."
- o **Ask for "feedforward"** – for two suggestions for the future that might help them achieve a positive change in their selected behavior. If you have worked with these people in the past, they are not allowed to give ANY feedback about the past. They are only allowed to give ideas for the future.
- o **Listen attentively to the suggestions and take notes.** You are not allowed to comment on the suggestions in any way. You are not allowed to critique the suggestions or even to make positive judgmental statements, such as, "That's a good idea."
- o **Thank** the other participants for their suggestions.
- o **Ask** the other person what they would like to change.
- o **Provide feedforward** - two suggestions aimed at helping the other person change.
- o **Say, "You are welcome."** when thanked for the suggestions. The entire process of both giving and receiving feedforward usually takes about two minutes.
- o **Find another person** and keep repeating the process until the exercise is stopped.

- When the exercise is finished, ask participants to provide one word that best describes their reaction to this experience. Complete the sentence, "This exercise was …". The words provided are almost always extremely positive, such as "great", "energizing", "useful" or "helpful." The most common word mentioned is "fun!" What is the last word that most of us think about when we receive feedback, coaching and developmental ideas? Fun!

- Adapted from "Try FeedForward Instead of Feedback," The Talent Strategy Group, adapted from Leader to Leader, Summer 2002, Marshall Goldsmith

IDENTIFY YOUR TOP STRENGTHS AND TOP AREAS FOR FURTHER DEVELOPMENT:

- Conduct a self-assessment of your leadership strengths and development needs.
  - o Create a "T-Chart" – on a blank piece of paper, draw a "T" covering the entire page.
  - o Label the column on the left "Towering Strengths" and the column on the right "Critical Development Areas."
  - o List under "Towering Strengths" the 3-5 capabilities or competencies that have been primarily responsible for your success to date.
  - o List under "Critical Development Areas" the 3-5 development areas that have tended to hold you back or have hindered your ability to be as successful as you would like to be.
  - o Discuss this chart with your direct manager or a trusted colleague and identify one area for development (Development Need/Opportunity) in mind that you want to work on, that you firmly believe that if you really learned and developed significantly more, faster in this area, that it would result in you performing at a higher level and creating greater value for yourself and your company as a result.
- Analyze Your Pivotal Learning Experiences
  - o The goal of this activity is to begin discovering who you are as a learner and how you came to be that way.
  - o Think back over the pivotal learning events in your life. These are experiences that had a significant impact on who you have become as a person and as a leader. Use the following questions to reflect on these experiences.
    - How did you get into the situation? What caused you to address the learning?

- What adjectives would you use to describe what you were feeling while you were immersed in the experience? Did your emotions change over time?

- What nuggets of insight or wisdom did you learn from this experience that you would pass on to someone else about to enter the same learning challenge?

- What was your learning process? How did you learn your way through the experience? What did you do to create or draw learning or meaning from the experience?

Self-Assessment: Score Yourself on Developing a Clear Understanding of Your Strengths and Areas of Development

Think about your work and life experiences over the past year and answer the following questions using this scale:

Never (1)   Rarely (2)   Sometimes (3)   Often (4)   Almost always (5)

- I take stock of my personality characteristics and how they influence my performance and behavior at work.   1   2   3   4   5

- I assess myself against the leadership competencies in the competency model of my organization.   1   2   3   4   5

- I ask others to help me by sharing their perspective on my strengths and areas for further development.   1   2   3   4   5

- I identify my top strengths and top areas for further development.   1   2   3   4   5

OVERALL SCORE:
Sum of Ratings divided by 4 (Number of Items)

Guide to Interpreting Your Overall Score

- If your overall score on this learning practice is 12 or less, consider taking more comprehensive action to gain an understanding of your strengths and areas for development as a leader. Refer to the Potential Developmental Actions for ideas on how you can make use of this Learning Practice to enhance your self-awareness.

- If your overall score on this learning practice is 13 to 17, you may already have some understanding of your strengths and areas for development. What can you do to obtain a deeper understanding of your personality characteristics and its impact on you as a leader? How can you gain a more complete understanding of your leadership competencies? Review the Potential Developmental Actions for ideas on how you can develop a better understanding of your strengths and areas of development.

- If your overall score on this learning practice is 18 or above, congratulations! You are actively engaged in leveraging feedback as a means of development. Remember that competency requirements change as organizations change, and leaders need to adapt to new conditions and demands as well!

REFLECTION QUESTIONS

What new strategic business challenges is your organization facing over the next 2-3 years?

Given those challenges, what new leadership competencies do you need to demonstrate in order to be aligned with the organization and the challenges it faces, and to be able to provide appropriate leadership?

How do you measure up against the new leadership competencies? Where are you strong and where do you need to improve?

What have you done in the last year to gain or maintain a clear understanding of your strengths and areas for development as a leader?

What have you done to increase your leadership competencies over the past year? Describe the actions you took and the results you have achieved so far.

Give an example of how you have helped others gain a clear understanding of their leadership strengths and areas for development.

What is your top priority development area at the present time? What is your plan to improve in this area? How will you know you have achieved success?

5. Ask Great Questions and Demonstrate Curiosity

"Learning depends on curiosity and asking questions. The experience of curiosity is equivalent to continuously living and operating out of a question frame as simple as "What's this?"—as all children do. It is through questions that we operationalize curiosity into behavior, and as a result they are the foundation of any kind of learning, be it formal, informal, or personal."

Michael J. Marquardt, <u>Leading with Questions</u>

Introduction

Why do you think developing as a leader depends so much on asking great questions and curiosity? Curiosity is one expression of being open-minded and having a Learning Mindset. Likewise, asking questions is a way of satisfying your curiosity about things you don't yet fully understand or desire to learn more about. As you reflect on your own level of curiosity and questioning skills, looks for opportunities to expand the types of questions you ask of others, and of yourself.

Review the list of behaviors, behavioral trends and patterns, and tendencies below. As you do, reflect on your own experience and try to recall specific situations or events that shed light on your own patterns of behavior related to this Learning Practice.

BEHAVIORS, BEHAVIORAL TRENDS AND PATTERNS, TENDENCIES:

- Ask open-ended questions to encourage people to expand their ideas and share them with you
- Ask probing questions in order to learn more about something
- Frame your questions positively
- Ask questions from the Learning Mindset, seeking to learn rather than to judge

Potential Developmental Actions

Review the following for examples of developmental actions you can take to enhance your effectiveness at asking great questions and demonstrating curiosity as a leader. Identify at least one or two actions that you will work to integrate into your day-to-day work life.

Types of Effective Questions

- Effective questions are questions that accomplish their purpose as well as build a positive relationship between the questioner and the person(s) being asked the questions. There are two broad types of questions: open-ended and closed questions. Closed questions seek a short, specific response, like yes or no. Open-ended questions give the person or group a great deal of freedom in deciding how to respond.

ASK OPEN-ENDED QUESTIONS TO ENCOURAGE PEOPLE TO EXPAND THEIR IDEAS AND SHARE THEM WITH YOU

- Open-ended questions encourage people to expand ideas and allow exploration of what's important to them or what is comfortable for them to reveal. They encourage people to do the work of self-reflection and problem solving rather than justifying or defending a position. Asking open-ended, unbiased questions also shows respect for the views of others. They help to establish rapport, gather information, and increase understanding.
    - Open-ended questions should begin with words like "why" and "how" or phrases such as "What do you think about..." Phrases to use with open-ended questions include:
        - What do you think about . . . ?
        - Could you say more about . . . ?
        - What possibilities come to mind . . . ?
        - What might happen if you . . . ?
        - What do you think you will lose if you give up (the point under discussion)?
        - What have you tried before?
        - What do you want to do next?

- **Why Questions.** Why questions are possibly the most important types of probing, open-ended questions for leaders to ask, because these questions force everyone to go into deeper layers of cause and effect, and of purposes and assumptions.

  - When asking "Why" questions, leaders should monitor their tone of voice, so that they don't convey anger or frustration, but instead curiosity and a search for knowledge or information.

  - **The "5 Whys"** is a fairly well known approach to asking "why" to solve questions. The essential idea is to ask "why" five times in an attempt to dig down to the core cause of a problem. It is especially useful to explore <u>systemic</u> issues and causes, and to avoid the trap of focusing on events or people. By the time you have asked "Why?" 5 times, chances are good that you will begin to see the problem or situation from a new perspective (see Senge's <u>The Fifth Discipline</u>). This process helps you:

    - Peel away the layers of symptoms

    - Quickly identify the root cause of a problem

    - Determine the relationship between different causes of a problem

    - When problems involve human factors or interactions

  - ***The "5 Whys" Process***

    - Take any problem and ask: *"Why is this occurring?"*

    - Answer the question.

    - Repeat the process five times, asking "why?" for every answer given in each cycle.

  - Be sure to reflect on your use of the "5 Whys" Process. Ask yourself the following questions:

    - What did I notice about asking why 5 times to uncover the causes of the problem?

    - How was using this technique different from the way I usually try to solve problems?

- What benefit do I see from using the 5 Whys Process?
- How can I use this more going forward to solve more problems more quickly and effectively?

FRAME YOUR QUESTIONS POSITIVELY

- Even if we have a strong desire to learn, our old habits can die hard. As leaders, we need to question our questions, and learn how to frame them effectively. According to Michael Marquardt (Leading With Questions, p. 83)):
  - "It is very easy when questioning to let our own values, preferences, and biases leak into what we are asking. We must develop the attitudes and skills to notice, analyze, and revise our questions. Before we ask a question, we should preview it in our minds from the other person's point of view to determine whether the question as phrased will be truly helpful. If you are unsure how a question might be taken, be frank and say so. For example, you might say, "I'm not sure how to ask this question, but . . .?" This is a way of defusing any issue that might arise from the way you ask a difficult question."

- Framing questions positively demonstrates interest in the other person's point of view, which is helpful in building relationships.
- It can also be useful to frame a question as a request for a favor: "I value your opinion highly, so I would appreciate it if you would tell me . . . " In this way, you ask for a gift rather than demanding something in a manner the other person may see as improper or threatening.
- The key to framing good questions is to think about the "quest" in your questions (Kouzes and Posner, 2002). What do you want this person to think about? What do you want to learn? A questing mindset shows that you care about the other person.

- Asking great questions is a powerful way to change the mindset of a team, because our mindsets can often be determined by the questions we ask. Some questions have the potential to create breakthrough thinking, while others lead to being stuck, stagnant, and demoralized. The key is to ask Learner Questions instead of Judger Questions (Marilee Adams, author of Change Your Questions, Change Your Life.)

- Learner questions are "open-minded, curious, and creative. They promote progress and possibilities, and typically lead to discoveries, understanding, and solutions. Judger questions are "more closed-minded, certain, and critical. They focus on problems rather than solutions and often lead to defensive reactions, negativity, and inertia. Learner questions facilitate progress by expanding options; Judger questions impede progress by limiting perspectives." (Marilee Adams, author of Change Your Questions, Change Your Life.)

- Leaders who cultivate a Learning Mindset tend to ask more Learner questions and, as a result, can improve their own and their team's performance and morale. In fact, when leaders shift into a Learning Mindset, they are more likely to recognize changes in employees' performance, and spend more time coaching, mentoring, and developing people.

- Review the two lists of questions below, to see the types of questions associated with the Learning Mindset and with the Judging Mindset:

Judging Questions	Learning Questions
• Who is to blame? Why can't they perform?	• What are my goals? What am I responsible for?
• How can I prove I'm right?	• What are the facts and what am I assuming?
• How can I protect my turf?	• How can I help?
• Why aren't we winning?	• What do our customers/stakeholders want?
• What could we lose?	• What steps can we take to improve the situation?
• Why bother?	• What's possible?

- Just knowing about the Learning Mindset and the importance of Asking Great Questions doesn't mean that it's easy to do. It can be very challenging because we are all so used to behaving in habitual patterns that are difficult to break. But remember: it is worth the effort to constantly work at enacting the Learning Mindset, by asking great questions. Teams that operate with a Learning Mindset are more productive, motivated and engaged.

- Take these steps to enacting the Learning Mindset through Asking Great Questions:
  - o **Work on your own mindset first.** Notice whether you are asking yourself Learning or Judging Questions, and the effect they have on your mood, engagement, and productivity. Then create Learning Questions that are focused on achieving your goals in specific areas. Is there an issue that you've been struggling with lately? Check to see if most of your focus has been on Judging Questions. If so, how can you switch to a Learning Mindset?

  - o **Elevate the quality of meetings.** Before any meeting you lead or attend, write down possible questions you could ask with a Learning focus, such as: What will it take to move this forward? Who has a possible solution for this? What is the best way to allocate our resources? You'll get the best solutions, and the fastest results, by asking the right questions.

  - o **Boost your team's energy, engagement, and productivity.** Notice the questions your team members typically ask, and the impact on morale, collaboration, problem solving, and results. Explain the Learning-Judging mindsets to your team, and then encourage them to focus more on Learner questions. Be sure you consistently model the Learner behaviors yourself and acknowledge your team as they begin to make the shift. Then, watch for ways that this increases their productivity, engagement, and results.

Top 12 Questions

- Use the "Top 12 Questions" (Marilee Adams, from the Inquiry Institute, http://inquiryinstitute.com/resources/top-12-questions/)

  - The questions on the Top 12 List evolved out of Marilee Adams' work with coaching clients and workshop participants over many years. The list can be used in at least three ways:

    - First, it is a logical sequence of questions to help you work through any situation you might want to change or improve.

    - Second, you might just want to scan the list for questions you've been missing.

    - Third, you can turn to it when you're looking for just the right question to emphasize in a particular situation.

  - Within this list are questions that are applicable to a variety of life's challenges. The goal is to integrate these questions into your everyday thinking. Then, when a challenge arises, you'll be able to easily recall some of them. Not every question applies to every situation. That's why you'll want to develop a collection of your favorites and work with them on a regular basis. These questions can open and change your mind. They allow you to unveil new choices, options, and possibilities you might otherwise have missed.

  - Here's the list:

    1. What do I want?
    2. What are my choices?
    3. What assumptions am I making?
    4. What am I responsible for?
    5. How else can I think about this?
    6. What is the other person thinking, feeling, needing, and wanting?
    7. What am I missing or avoiding?
    8. What can I learn?
       - From this person or situation?
       - From this mistake or failure?

- From this success?
  9. What action steps make the most sense?
  10. What questions should I ask (myself or others?)
  11. How can I turn this into a win-win?
  12. What is possible?
  - Keep this list in a handy place where you can refer to it whenever you feel stuck, want new alternatives, or a change.

Question-Storming Instead of Brainstorming

- Leaders often use Brainstorming as a technique to generate lots of ideas to solve problems. Regular brainstorming for ideas often hits a wall because we only have so many ideas, and the reason we hit that wall is we're asking the wrong questions. We could be sitting in a meeting discussing an issue that we all care about, it matters to us, we've wrestled with it, we've debated it, we've struggled with it, we have done our homework on it, but we're hitting heads and we are just going nowhere in the conversation or in team meeting. When people care about the issue, when they have thought a lot about the issue, but they are stuck, that's the perfect time to step back and say: Okay, question storming time.
- What is Question-Storming? If you're with a team, do this:
  - Grab a flip chart.
  - Have someone be the scribe and have the team generate at least 50 questions about the problem that we're stuck on.
  - Number the questions. Write them down up there, when they are being written down other team members are paying attention and thinking of a better question.
  - Do it again and again and again. At about question 25, it will stall. People will say 'I don't have any more questions, I am stuck.' Keep going. Because it's that pass forward that can sometimes give you some of the greatest questions.
  - And if you really are devoted to the problem and you want to get a solution, go for 75 questions, not 50.

- When people step back and do that kind of question storming, collectively list a long series of questions where they can see the questions and generate new ones, it actually gets them closer to the right question that will give them the right answer.
- Source: Hal Gregersen, Question-Storming vs. Brainstorming, http://vimeo.com/48200106

Q-Storming – Another Variation on the Theme

- Q-Storming is most often used when breakthroughs are desired in decision making, problem solving, strategic planning, and innovation. It is a tool for moving beyond limitations in perception and thinking and advancing to novel and extraordinary solutions and answers. While Q-Storming is similar to brainstorming, the goal of this practice is to generate as many questions as possible. The expectation is that some of these questions will provide desired new openings or directions. Typically, questions open thinking, while answers often close thinking.
- Q-Storming is based on three premises: (1) Great results begin with great questions; (2) Most any problem can be solved with enough of the right questions; and (3) The questions we ask ourselves often provide the most fruitful openings for new thinking and possibilities. Q-Storming is typically done with a group or team, especially when exploring ideas and possibilities. It is also used in goal-oriented conversations between two people, for example, in coaching, leadership, management, or sales. Q-Storming can be done in person or virtually, with a global team or a coaching client in a different geographic location.
- The facilitator focuses on developing a robust goal and eliciting assumptions about it prior to the question-generation phase of Q-Storming. Often at the end, action plans will be made or revised based on discoveries made during the Q-Storming session.

Q-Storming Question Guidelines

- Questions should be first person singular or plural, using "I" and "we." You want new questions *to think with*, not necessarily to ask someone else.
- Generate questions from the Learning Mindset, and avoid Judging questions.

- Questions are mostly open-ended, not closed ("How can I?" rather than "Can I?" and "How can we?" rather than "Can you?")
- Invite courageous and provocative, as well as "silly" and "dumb" questions.
- Source: Marilee Adams, http://inquiryinstitute.com/resources/q-storming/

NOTE: Q-Storming is a powerful tool for creative thinking. However, use of Q-Storming for complex or challenging issues may be best supported by professional facilitation.

NOTE: To learn more about leading with questions, see Bob Tiede's website www.leadingwithquestions.com, and follow his blog.

Use of Questions in "Action Learning"

- Action Learning, created by Professor Reg Revans in the 1940s at the Cavendish Lab at Cambridge University, is a process in which participants learn by doing. Action Learning consists of the following key elements:
  - A real problem, challenge, or task
  - A group of 4 - 8 diverse, committed people
  - Use of *reflective questioning and listening*
  - Commitment and accountability for action
  - Focus and commitment to learning
- In solving organizational or individual leadership challenges, participants enhance their leadership capabilities and maturity. Research and experience tells us that Action Learning programs are far more effective than traditional training.
- *NOTE:* Action Learning is a powerful tool for leadership development, and relies heavily on a specific, facilitated approach to asking questions and interacting to solve challenging problems. Because of this, it is best supported by professional facilitation and coaching.

Self-Assessment: Score Yourself on Asking Great Questions / Curiosity

Think about your work and life experiences over the past year and answer the following questions using this scale:

Never (1)   Rarely (2)   Sometimes (3)   Often (4)   Almost always (5)

- I ask open-ended questions to encourage people to expand their ideas and share them with me.   1   2   3   4   5

- I ask probing questions in order to learn more about something.   1   2   3   4   5

- I frame my questions positively.   1   2   3   4   5

- I ask questions from the Learning Mindset, seeking to learn rather than judge.   1   2   3   4   5

OVERALL SCORE:
Sum of Ratings divided by 4 (Number of Items)

Guide to Interpreting Your Overall Score

- If your overall score on this learning practice is 12 or less, think about how you can demonstrate genuine curiosity and ask great questions. Learn everything you can about questions and how to use them for learning, growth and development. Refer to the following Potential Developmental Actions for ideas on how you can more effectively integrate this Learning Practice into your work life.

- If your overall score on this learning practice is 13 to 17, you are already using questions to your benefit. What can you do to sharpen your use of great questions for developmental purposes? Think about ways you can increase your use of questions every day. Review the Potential Developmental Actions for ideas on how you can use questions as a development tool.

- If your overall score on this learning practice is 18 or above, congratulations! Maintaining a Learning Mindset is an on-going journey. Take your curiosity and question-asking skills to the next level!

REFLECTION QUESTIONS

Reflect on the past year and identify a situation in which you effectively used questions as a leadership skill. What was the situation? How did you use questions to obtain an outcome? What types of questions did you use? Why was your use of questions especially effective?

Describe a situation in which you observed someone other than yourself skillfully and effectively use questions to achieve an important leadership outcome. What was the situation? How did they use questions to obtain that outcome? What types of questions did they use? Why was their use of questions especially effective?

What is one concrete example of you not using effective questions as a leader? What was the situation? What did you do? Why was the exchange ineffective? What did you learn as a result of this situation?

What have you done in the last year to improve your effectiveness at asking questions?

How have you coached colleagues or others to help them develop greater skills and effectiveness at asking great questions?

How do you express curiosity as a leader?

6. Listen Transformatively

"The best advice I ever heard about listening—advice that significantly changed my own approach—came from Sam Palmisano, when he was talking to our leadership team. Someone asked him why his experience working in Japan was so important to his leadership development, and he said, "Because I learned to listen." And I thought, "That's pretty amazing." He also said, "I learned to listen by having only one objective: comprehension. I was only trying to understand what the person was trying to convey to me. I wasn't listening to critique or object or convince."[8]

Kevin Sharer, CEO Amgen

Introduction

Transformative Listening is a journey. You have to practice it. Every day. Forever. And, it evolves to higher levels as you do so. It is about being there for your conversation partner. It is an act of generosity. You give the gift of your presence to another. You set aside your narrative, its perceptions, beliefs and judgments. You leave room for silence. You never interrupt. You offer no advice, unless asked. You allow your partner to hear their own words, to further explore his meaning, to be safe and not contradicted for as long as necessary. Then, and only then, is your partner prepared to listen to you. Transformative listening deepens the conversation. It honors the speaker. It grows the relationship. It allows for greater understanding and creativity. Practice Transformative Listening so that your work with others can proceed from a more fundamental level of understanding and engagement.

Review the list of behaviors, behavioral trends and patterns, and tendencies below. As you do, reflect on your own experience and try to recall specific situations or events that shed light on your own patterns of behavior related to this Learning Practice.

---

[8] Why I'm a Listener: Amgen CEO Kevin Sharer. McKinsey, 2012.

BEHAVIORS, BEHAVIORAL TRENDS AND PATTERNS, TENDENCIES:

- Listen to others with the Learning Mindset, seeking to learn rather than to judge
- Listen to explore your own perceptions, filters, and biases, and become aware of how they affect your behavior
- Listen intently, deeply, empathically
- Listen to understand both the content and the affect of the speaker
- Listen to grasp the intentions and deeper purpose of the speaker, i.e., what they want to achieve

Potential Developmental Actions

Try to identify one or two actions that you will work to integrate into your day-to-day work life.

LISTEN TO OTHERS WITH THE LEARNING MINDSET, SEEKING TO LEARN RATHER THAN TO JUDGE

- Practice Mindful Attention to the person to whom you are listening. Make a conscious choice to let conversation flow from your partner. Hold yourself in reserve, but don't just focus on "air time," or trying to maintain a balance of how much you talk and how much they talk. Hold yourself to 10% of air time or less, and use your words to help the other person take their thinking deeper. Ask questions such as "Why do you think that happened?" "How did it make you feel?" "What did you learn from the experience?"
- Transformative Listening is in large part Mindful Listening. "Both mindful speech and mindful listening can be taught and practiced, like any skill... Both involve attending to another person with full attention while being aware of your own 'self' (body, thought, and emotion) so as not to react without clear forethought."[9] Smalley and Winston recommend that we practice both mindful speaking and mindful listening. Try this Transformative Listening Exercise to learn about and develop your ability to speak and listen mindfully. It could well transform you as a leader.
    - Enlist a friend for this exercise. Alternate between speaking and listening. Decide who will speak first. That person then practices mindfulness while speaking without being interrupted for two minutes (set a timer). The speaker can pick a topic of interest to him

---

[9] <u>Fully Present: The Science, Art, and Practice of Mindfulness</u>. Smalley & Winston. Da Capo Press, 2010.

or her, such as, "What brings me joy?"

- o The other listens mindfully, practicing the following:
  - ▪ Noticing his or her body from time to time
  - ▪ Noticing his or her thoughts and reactions from time to time
  - ▪ Most importantly, trying hard to offer complete attention to the speaker
- o The mindful speaker practices the following:
  - ▪ Noticing his or her body from time to time
  - ▪ Articulating what he or she is aware of from time to time
  - ▪ Speaking authentically and from the heart
- o At the end of two minutes, both of you close your eyes and check into yourselves to see how it felt to do this exercise. Then reverse. At the end of two more minutes, close your eyes again and check in with yourselves.
- o For a third time, have a conversation about the experience of doing the exercise and follow up with any questions or reflections you may have for your partner.

"I really developed, as my own personal success approach, so to speak, is, early on listen, and give the people the feeling that they are valued, that you as a person value them, and value what they have to say. And I've experienced that this developed a very trustful relationship within a very short period of time."

Global Leader, in How Global Leaders Develop, 2010

LISTEN TO EXPLORE YOUR OWN PERCEPTIONS, FILTERS, AND BIASES, AND BECOME AWARE OF HOW THEY AFFECT YOUR BEHAVIOR

- Transformative Listening is not passive, it is active engagement. "It requires making yourself available, free from judgments and beliefs. It requires empathy, which means you must overcome your self-centeredness, your personality, and your narrative. It demands that you exist, for the period of the listening engagement, for the benefit of the speaker. It insists that you be available for whatever is communicated, no matter how potentially disagreeable, upsetting, incongruous or hurtful, it may be."

- "Transformative Listening requires certain qualities of strength, endurance and discipline to master. And, in many cases, it may require the acknowledgement of failure and a renewed dedication to becoming available again and again, even in the course of a single conversation."

- "Finally, Transformative Listening does not just engage your ears and mind. It requires focused attention on your body, heart, gut and 'spirit,' all while engaging the speech, facial expressions, body postures and movements, and emotions of the speaker." [10]

LISTEN INTENTLY, DEEPLY, EMPATHICALLY

LISTEN TO UNDERSTAND BOTH THE CONTENT AND THE AFFECT OF THE SPEAKER

LISTEN TO GRASP THE INTENTIONS AND DEEPER PURPOSE OF THE SPEAKER, I.E., WHAT THEY WANT TO ACHIEVE

Effective Dialogue

- "Dialogue is the basic unit of work in an organization." – Ram Charan, Conquering a Culture of Indecision. Since dialogue is the basic unit of work, a leader is influencing work even when she or he is not in the room. What is the conversation that goes on after you leave the room? When we improve the quality of conversation, we improve outcomes and results. The quality of interactions between people determines alignment, action, commitment, and adjustment. Leaders who take on the mastery of valuable dialogue can use those interactions to produce more valuable results with less time, money, and stress. When managers struggle to have adequate resources and face tight budgets, why leave money on the table?

- Dialogue is – at its most basic level – a meaningful conversation or exchange between two individuals. It involves two "common" skills that are not commonly used very well: Listening and Asking Questions. We can improve the effectiveness of our dialogue if we pay attention to a number of key ingredients: tools and techniques that can reduce stress, save time, save money, improve relationships and add value.

---

[10] "Transformative Listening: Invigorating Your Life With Each Conversation, www.mckennalong.com/publications-689.html.

- The consulting company Conversant developed the "Effective Dialogue" model, and it is described in their book <u>The Communication Catalyst</u>. The essence of their model is this:
  - "High-performance conversation is not about being glib. It is not spin control. It is not limited to emotional intelligence, because conversational intelligence includes emotions and much more. High-performance conversation is well-designed listening and speaking that creates high-velocity value. Remember our definition of value: What customers and investors are willing to pay for, that employees are willing and able to provide. You can accelerate that kind of value if you:
    - Understand a useful model for how conversations affect perceptions, priorities, and action.
    - Apply the model to any current challenge that requires you to coordinate different interests.
    - Measure the results.
    - Use the model to debrief, learn, and adjust.
  - The Communication Catalyst provides a conversational model, which we call the cycle of value. The cycle of value promotes teamwork, creativity, planning, accountability, and learning; we also address how those same things break down. Use the cycle of value well, and you will accelerate achievement and prevent a multitude of mistakes. The three-part cycle of value:
    1. **Align** conversations create shared purpose, stimulate creativity, and ensure smart planning.
    2. **Act** conversations clarify accountabilities and launch action.
    3. **Adjust** conversations review performance and translate experience into improvement.
  - When these three related elements are effective, work is meaningful, satisfying, and fast. We infuse work with meaning, galvanize teams, and inflame loyalty among customers, employees, and investors. When these elements are ineffective, we decelerate our high-speed ambitions. We render work meaningless, destroy

teamwork, and inflame discontent among customers, employees, and investors.

- o If you take the time to understand and apply our conversational cycle of value, we promise you will see measurable results. The cycle includes aligning the interests of employees, customers, and investors, so conversational leadership will ultimately effect three measures:
    - Attraction and retention of valuable people (employees perceive value)
    - Profitable revenue (customers perceive value)
    - Investor return (shareowners perceive value)
- o You also can see the benefit in other measurable areas when you apply the architecture. Decreased time-to-market, increased customer loyalty, and increased earnings-per-share are examples.
- o If you are responsible for coordinating the efforts of others, you are a prime candidate for The Communication Catalyst. To find out for sure, answer "yes" or "no" to these six questions:
    1. Do you think it's important to increase the rate of achievement around you?
    2. Are you unsure how to accelerate things to your satisfaction?
    3. Are you interested in accelerating your learning curve by profiting from others' mistakes, victories, and lessons?
    4. Are you frustrated by not getting others to adopt the attitudes and practices that you know would improve performance?
    5. Do you believe that the conversations you have with stakeholders (e.g., customers, employees, executives, board members, allies, and shareowners) are important to value creation?
    6. Are you willing to question your own habits and beliefs and explore new ones to speed business success?
- o If you answered "yes" to four or more questions, The Communication Catalyst is well worth your time and money. If you said "yes" to all six questions, it would be wise to make The Communication Catalyst an immediate priority. If you answered "no" to most

or all of the questions, then do not read The Communication Catalyst."

- o Training in the art of Effective Dialogue and the tools and skills presented in The Communication Catalyst is available from Aspire Consulting and Conversant, Inc.

- o To learn more about Effective Dialogue, read <u>The Communication Catalyst</u>, by Mickey Connolly and Richard Rianoshek, 2002, Kaplan Publishing.

Self-Assessment: Score Yourself on Transformative Listening

Think about your work and life experiences over the past year and answer the following questions using this scale:

Never (1)　　　　Rarely (2)　　　　Sometimes (3)　　　　Often (4)　　　　Almost always (5)

- I listen to others with the Learning Mindset, seeking to learn rather than to judge.   **1 2 3 4 5**

- I listen to explore my own perceptions, filters, and biases, and become aware of how they affect my behavior.   **1 2 3 4 5**

- I listen intently, deeply, and empathically.   **1 2 3 4 5**

- I listen to understand both the content and the affect of the speaker.   **1 2 3 4 5**

- I listen to grasp the intentions and deeper purpose of the speaker, i.e., what they want to achieve.   **1 2 3 4 5**

OVERALL SCORE:
Sum of Ratings divided by 5 (Number of Items)

Guide to Interpreting Your Overall Score

- If your overall score on this learning practice is 15 or less, think about how you can increase both the quality and quantity of listening. Are there specific types of situations where you find it difficult to listen? How do colleagues or family members perceive you as a listener? What can you do to change your own and others' perceptions that you need to improve in this area? Refer to the Potential Developmental Actions for ideas on how you can become a better listener.

- If your overall score on this learning practice is 16 to 20, you are already using it to learn, grow and develop. How can you become a transformational listener? What can you do to develop a reputation as someone who is a great listener? How can you listen more effectively in order to accelerate your development? Review the Potential Developmental Actions for ideas on how you can listen more effectively.

- If your overall score on this learning practice is 21 or above, congratulations! You are using one of the most powerful of all learning practices to grow and develop as a leader. Be careful not to overestimate your ability with this one; it's very easy to see yourself as much more effective at this than others do. To keep sharp, ask others how they see you at transformative listening.

REFLECTION QUESTIONS

Why is it important to listen to others to understand both the content of what they say as well as the "affect" contained in their words?

How important is it to listen to grasp the intentions and deeper purpose of someone, instead of the surface level of their words?

Describe a time when you purposely listened to someone at work intently, deeply, and empathically? What did you do that was different or unique from other interactions? What was the outcome of the interaction?

Think about a time when you listened to others with a Learning Mindset (i.e., open-minded, focused on learning not judging, curious, exploratory, etc.). What was the situation? Who were you listening to? What growth or change did you experience as a result? What impact did listening in that way have on the person you listened to?

What have you done in the last year to improve your listening capabilities?

How do you maintain awareness of your own skills as a listener?

7. Respond to Experiences with Adaptability and Flexibility

"In a high operational tempo, it is critical to adapt and to be flexible. It is a delicate dance. One must adapt and be flexible in a smart manner pending on context of the situation. The flexibility must be for the optimal performance of the group, organization or agency. If in a time sensitive life or death situation, the context defines the limits of adaptability and flexibility."

Dr. Dolores Manley, Independent Consultant

INTRODUCTION

Conditions of the business world today are perfectly described by an acronym that was coined by the U.S. military in the late 1990's to describe the post-Cold War world: VUCA. VUCA stands for Volatility, Uncertainty, Complexity, and Ambiguity. It took hold as an acronym after the terrorist attacks of September 2001, and business leaders have since then adopted it to describe today's business environment.

In a VUCA world, leaders need to be more adaptable and flexible than ever in order to remain effective in such a volatile, unpredictable environment. Research by the Boston Consulting Group and the Center for Leadership Development indicate that organizations and leaders need to develop more complex and adaptive thinking and acting abilities. Although the need for high levels of flexibility and adaptability is clear, developing and demonstrating these capabilities can be challenging.

Given the increasing importance of adaptability and flexibility, you may want to focus your attention on getting better at demonstrating them. Our Learning Mindset model, which emerged from our research into how global leaders develop, emphasizes the importance of learning from experience in dynamic and changing situations. Adopting and sustaining a learning mindset leads to being adaptable and flexible in new, volatile circumstances. As you respond to experience with adaptability and flexibility you naturally reinforce your learning mindset, because you experience the benefits of being adaptable and flexible that, in turn, generates better outcomes along with increased curiosity.

Adaptability shows that you can readily adjust to new situations and respond well to changing circumstances. The opposite characteristic – rigidity or inflexibility – contributes to leadership failure and derailment. It is even more important to be adaptable and flexible when operating in an environment of rapid, frequent change.

Review the list of behaviors, behavioral trends and patterns, and tendencies below. As you do, reflect on your own experience and try to recall specific situations or events that shed light on your own patterns of behavior related to this Learning Practice.

BEHAVIORS, BEHAVIORAL TRENDS AND PATTERNS, TENDENCIES:

- Change your behavior according to the situation at hand
- Resist the tendency to use "muscle memory" (old, familiar ways of leading and acting) and proactively choose your actions depending on the circumstance
- Don't insist on your own way, even when you have "been there, done that" and think you know the "right" way
- Solicit others' ideas about how to handle situations, especially those from different cultural backgrounds

Potential Developmental Actions

Review the following for examples of developmental actions you can take to enhance your effectiveness at responding to experiences with adaptability and flexibility, so that you learn, grow and develop as a leader. Identify at least one or two actions that you will work to integrate into your day-to-day work life.

CHANGE YOUR BEHAVIOR ACCORDING TO THE SITUATION AT HAND:

- Every situation requires slightly different skills and approaches. It is up to you to assess the situation and people involved, and adapt to effectively respond. Consider the following suggestions.
    - Think of someone who you believe is very flexible and an effective leader. Watch closely how they lead in a few situations, and observe how others react to their leadership styles

and behaviors. If you see them doing something that seems to be effective, incorporate that leadership behavior into your own style if it makes sense for you.

- o Go directly to your direct reports and peers, and ask them to give you 3 ideas on what you could do to more effectively adapt your leadership style. Make sure you take a notebook with you so you can write down what they say. Don't try to defend or explain yourself; that will stop you from listening and will create the impression that you don't really want to hear what they have to say anyway. Your only job is to listen to what they say, write down what they say, and then say "Thank you!"

- Become a Change Agent
    - o Stay ahead of changes in your organization. The more information you have about what is happening, and what is likely to happen, the better prepared you will be to handle the stress associated with change.
    - o Take a step back from the change and analyze it to identify opportunities. Consider using a SWOT (Strengths, Weaknesses, Opportunities, Threats) matrix to help your team map out their view of the change.

> *"I think, in terms of shaping me from a leadership standpoint, it's shaped me from a learning agility perspective, realizing that this could broaden your mind to keep yourself open to these things, and this may sound odd, but I even find that now I try to read much more broadly than I did before just to open myself up to different fields, different types of books that really got me going in terms of thinking these things out...and I think it's around adaptability, flexibility, and the richness that you can get from that."*
>
> **Global Leader, in How Global Leaders Develop, 2010**

RESIST THE TENDENCY TO USE OLD, FAMILIAR WAYS OF LEADING AND PROACTIVELY CHOOSE YOUR ACTIONS DEPENDING ON THE CIRCUMSTANCE:

- Conditions of the business world today are perfectly described by an acronym that was coined by the U.S. military in the late 1990's to describe the post-Cold War world: VUCA. VUCA stands for Volatility, Uncertainty, Complexity, and Ambiguity. It took hold as an acronym after the terrorist attacks of September, 2001, and it has been adopted by business leaders to describe today's business environment.

- In a VUCA world, leaders need to be more adaptable and flexible than ever in order to remain effective in such a volatile, unpredictable environment. Research by the Boston Consulting Group and the Center for Leadership Development indicate that organizations and leaders need to develop more complex and adaptive thinking and acting abilities. Although the need for high levels of flexibility and adaptability is clear, developing and demonstrating these capabilities can be challenging. Review the following tips and tactics to develop increased flexibility and adaptability in challenging and/or changing situations.

- Shake Up Your Routine: Take a new route to work, just to have different scenery. Listen to a new type of music, and learn to appreciate styles of music you are unfamiliar with; possibly learn how to play a musical instrument. Read a completely different genre of literature, and become familiar with bodies of knowledge that are extremely different from your day-to-day thought life.

- Be flexible when working with others. Remember that there are many ways of getting things done, and that there may not be one best way. Work with others to jointly define deliverables. Ask trusted co-workers to tell you when they think you are being inflexible . . . And be prepared to hear some surprising answers. Make it a point to adapt to others' preferences and styles. You may be surprised at the benefits this yields.

- Be flexible in how you view situations. If you are used to seeing things a certain way, you may have limited yourself with mental "blinders."

DON'T INSIST ON YOUR OWN WAY, EVEN WHEN YOU HAVE "BEEN THERE, DONE THAT" AND THINK YOU KNOW THE "RIGHT" WAY:

Overcome Established Behavior Patterns

- One of the main challenges in responding to experiences with adaptability and flexibility is **overcoming established behavior patterns and perspectives**. If you find yourself automatically responding to certain kinds of situations or people, the first step is to identify and acknowledge that you may be reacting without fully understanding the situation or on the basis of past events or interactions. These knee-jerk reactions may have become involuntary, and you may not even be aware that you're responding that way. To increase your awareness of how you respond to challenging situations and people, consider some of the following suggestions:

  - If you have recently completed a personality assessment tool, such as the Hogan Personality Inventory, the Myers-Briggs Type Indicator, or another instrument, review the results of the assessment to identify any personality characteristics or behavioral patterns that shed light on your typical ability to be flexible and adaptable. Think about these questions:

    - Do you tend to demonstrate a pattern of behavior that is closed to others, or more open to others?

    - Do you prefer a high degree of structure and plans, or are you more comfortable with less structure and less formal plans?

    - How do these behavioral patterns and tendencies relate to your ability to demonstrate flexibility and adaptability on the job?

  - Think about how you typically handle situations. Ask colleagues, peers, or family members who see you in a range of circumstances. Try to determine if you generally treat all situations the same and apply the same solutions or responses, or if you tailor your response to events. Do you tend to see "shades of gray" or do you see things as "black-and-white?" If you tend to see things as "black-and-white," how can you broaden or open up your perspective to see situations with more nuance or complexity?

o When you face a new situation, compare it to other situations you have faced. How is it similar or different? What familiar approaches can you build on? If necessary, how can you create a completely new solution?

o When you encounter opinions or approaches that are different from your own, try to adopt a more flexible approach that can blend elements of your thoughts and approaches with those of others. Remember that you might be so used to seeing something from your own perspective that you just can't see any other possibilities. Suspend your judgment and engage in an open discussion where you focus only on listening to understand the other person's point of view.

o Ask your co-workers to tell you when they think you are being inflexible or rigid in response to others' ideas. Prepare yourself to receive information that might be difficult to hear, but listen carefully without defending or explaining yourself. Thank them for sharing their perspective, and then reflect on what they told you. Ask yourself "What can I learn about myself from their comments?" and "As a result of what I heard and learned about myself, what do I want to do differently going forward?"

Demonstrate Receptiveness to New Ideas

- **Manage your reactions to other people.** If someone takes a stand on something that you disagree with, resist the urge to attack their logic. Instead, draw the speaker out by asking Learning questions and other great questions. Make sure you understand the other person, and convey to them that you understand and appreciate their position, **before** you respond by sharing your thoughts or opinions. When you do respond, use "tentative" language such as "The part that I need to understand better is . . ." or "The piece that I am a bit concerned about is . . ."

Demonstrate Composure and Patience

- The amount of change many leaders experience in organizations today is accompanied by a high level of stress. When you're under stress, you may find that you react more quickly or more intensely than you normally do. This can make it challenging and difficult for you and your colleagues (both direct reports and higher level leaders) to work together effectively. Consider the following suggestions to help you maintain your composure while also being flexible and adaptable.

- o When you get angry, slow down, take a deep breath and stop yourself before you say something you'll regret.

- o Think before you speak. If you are upset or angry, let the emotion subside or drain away before you say something or send an email. When our emotions are high, we can't think clearly or rationally, and we may take an action that seems perfectly reasonable and logical to us right them. But later, when we re-read that email, or start replaying our words back to ourselves, we may discover that we have acted or spoken too quickly, or made an error in judgment.

- o If losing your composure or temper is a problem for you, make a list of your own personal signals, the things that you can look for so you know you are close to losing your composure; things like tunnel vision, rapid pulse, shallow breathing, constriction in your chest, clenched jaw, etc. Make it a point to become aware of these symptoms of "losing it" and then when you become aware, let it go: take a walk, listen to some soothing music, or take some other action that lets the energy dissipate.

- o You can also enlist the help of your friends and colleagues to manage this issue. Having someone to vent your frustrations to, who will listen and support you, can be very valuable.

> *"I am often in situations that are new, where I don't know all I need to know, so being open and flexible is key to success. . . I found out the hard way when I was working in global health, that I was blind to the degree of differences that others might have from the way I see the world and the practices I value. As a result, I am much more open to adapting to others rather than insisting on my own way as the best way."*
>
> **Margaret McIntyre, Independent Consultant**

Don't Insist On Your Own Way

- Organizations have many competing priorities, and leaders certainly experience the stress created by this situation. In every organization there will be competing opinions, priorities, agendas, personalities, goals, and ideas about how to achieve goals. It's completely reasonable to understand that you won't always get things "your way." The problem is, we are not completely reasonable creatures: we also have a powerful emotional side as well, and when we encounter frustrations we feel stress and a range of emotional reactions.

- If you're not careful, the stress can overcome your ability to respond with flexibility and adaptability when your great idea is rejected, or your opinion is ignored or put to the side instead of being action upon. When you experience this frustration or rejection, try some of these suggestions on how to respond to experience with flexibility and adaptability:

  - Even though you may not be able to control a situation, you can still control your emotions and other reactions. You can decide how you will feel about what happens, about what other people say, and about how you are treated. This is Self-Management, an important element of Emotional Intelligence, in which you exercise emotional self-control, maintain your integrity, and demonstrate flexibility in handling change and challenging situations.

  - Remember that you don't see the whole picture, and that someone else who you may believe is deliberately frustrating you actually has a different, and entirely legitimate perspective on the situation. Take the time to become aware of your own emotions and recognize how the emotions are affecting your behavior and performance. Take positive action to understand the other person's point of view, and step back to analyze the entire situation. Remember to use Social Awareness as well, especially empathy so you can sense the other person's feelings and perspectives.

  - Adjust your expectations. It's not reasonable to expect that others will always agree with you, or that you will always get what you want. Be prepared to not insist on your own way, even when you have "been there, done that" and think you know the "right" way. Accept that the world is the way it is, and move on.

- Leaders who have a Learning Mindset intentionally gain something positive from every experience they have. Ask yourself a few Learning Questions:
  - What can I learn from this situation?
  - What have I been doing that created this situation?
  - What did I do that seemed to work well? Not so well?
  - What would I do differently if I ever had the chance to do it again?
- Even "negative" or difficult experiences can be worthwhile if you purposely and intentionally learn from them. Remember, this situation may not appear to be valuable or important today, but it could provide you with an important perspective or skill that is extremely valuable in the future.

SOLICIT OTHERS' IDEAS ABOUT HOW TO HANDLE SITUATIONS, ESPECIALLY THOSE FROM DIFFERENT CULTURAL BACKGROUNDS:

- Go directly to your direct reports, peers, and other colleagues, and ask them to give you 3 ideas on what you could do to more effectively adapt your leadership style. Make sure you take a notebook with you so you can write down what they say. Don't try to defend or explain yourself; that will stop you from listening and will create the impression that you don't really want to hear what they have to say anyway. Your only job is to listen to what they say, write down what they say, and then say "Thank you!"
- If you have a challenging situation to deal with and you're not sure how to handle it, do your best to analyze the situation objectively and then ask a colleague to help you identify at least three ways to handle the situation.
- Work with a colleague to learn about and develop your ability to speak and listen mindfully, through the exercise "Transformative Listening Exercise" (this is the same exercise found in the previous chapter, to reinforce the importance of this Learning Practice):

Transformative Listening Exercise[11]

Transformative listening is not passive; it is active engagement. It requires focused attention on your body, heart, gut and 'spirit,' all while engaging the words, facial expressions, body postures and movements, and emotions of the speaker.

In this exercise, work with a colleague to learn about and develop your ability to speak and listen mindfully. You will alternate between speaking and listening.

1. Decide who will speak first. That person then practices mindfulness while speaking without being interrupted for two minutes (set a timer). The speaker can pick a topic of interest to him or her, such as, "What brings me joy?"
2. The other listens mindfully, practicing the following:
   - Noticing his or her body from time to time
   - Noticing his or her thoughts and reactions from time to time
   - Most importantly, trying hard to offer complete attention to the speaker
3. The mindful speaker practices the following:
   - Noticing his or her body from time to time
   - Articulating what he or she is aware of from time to time
   - Speaking authentically and from the heart
4. At the end of two minutes, both of you close your eyes and check into yourselves to see how it felt to do this exercise. Then reverse. At the end of two more minutes, close your eyes again and check in with yourselves.
5. For a third time, have a conversation about the experience of doing the exercise and follow up with any questions or reflections you may have for your partner.

---

[11] Source unknown.

After completing the Transformative Listening Exercise described above, use one of the reflection techniques covered in this Guide, such as Scaffolded Reflection ("What, So What, Now What?") to derive insights and new knowledge from the exercise.

Self-Assessment: Score Yourself on Responding to Experiences with Adaptability and Flexibility

Think about your work and life experiences over the past year and answer the following questions using this scale:

| Never (1) | Rarely (2) | Sometimes (3) | Often (4) | Almost always (5) |

- I change my behavior according to the situation at hand.   **1   2   3   4   5**

- I resist the tendency to use "muscle memory" (old, familiar ways of leading and acting) and proactively choose my actions depending on the circumstances.   **1   2   3   4   5**

- I don't insist on my own way, even when I have "been there, done that" and think I know the "right" way.   **1   2   3   4   5**

- I solicit others' ideas about how to handle situations, especially those from different cultural backgrounds.   **1   2   3   4   5**

OVERALL SCORE:
Sum of Ratings divided by 4 (Number of Items)

Guide to Interpreting Your Overall Score

- If your overall score on this learning practice is 12 or less, think about how you can become more adaptable as situations change. What can you do to break out of old patterns and do something different? What is one behavior in this learning practice that you could change that would have a significant impact on your learning and development as a leader? Refer to the Potential Developmental Actions for ideas on how you can more effectively integrate this Learning Practice into your work life.

- If your overall score on this learning practice is 13 to 17, you are already demonstrating adaptability and flexibility in some areas of your work life. What can you do to intentionally and consciously increase your use of these behaviors to foster your own development? Think about ways you can develop new "muscle memory" to acquire habits of mind that emphasize flexibility and adaptability. Review the Potential Developmental Actions for ideas on how you can develop increase ability to respond to experience with adaptability and flexibility.

- If your overall score on this learning practice is 18 or above, congratulations! Look for every opportunity to exhibit adaptability and flexibility. Keep it up!

REFLECTION QUESTIONS

What challenges are you dealing with that test your flexibility and adaptability?

How can you resist the tendency to rely on your old habits or "muscle memory" and respond to difficult challenges with flexibility and adaptability?

How would your colleagues describe you? Flexible or inflexible? Adaptable or unchanging?

What is one concrete example of you not being flexible and adaptable? How did that impact your learning, growth, and development as a leader?

How do you coach and mentor your colleagues to demonstrate adaptability and flexibility?

Describe a time when you solicited ideas about how to handle difficult situations from people with different cultural backgrounds than yours. How did you frame the request? How did they respond?

8. Active Reflection / Mindfulness

"By three methods we may learn wisdom: First, by reflection, which is noblest; Second, by imitation, which is easiest; and third by experience which is bitterest."

Confucius

Introduction

The transformation of experience into learning and meaning comes about through active and repeated reflection. Reflection prevents us from having 1 year of experience 20 times, and helps us gain learning, growth, and development from our experience. Essentially, reflection is thinking back on what we have done in order to discover how what we did led to the outcomes that we achieved, positive and/or negative. How can you use the insights and new knowledge you gain from reflection to plan for improved performance in the future?

Review the list of behaviors, behavioral trends and patterns, and tendencies below. As you do, reflect on your own experience and try to recall specific situations or events that shed light on your own patterns of behavior related to this Learning Practice.

BEHAVIORS, BEHAVIORAL TRENDS AND PATTERNS, TENDENCIES

- Take the time to reflect on and think about situations you have been in at work, what your behavior was, how you were feeling, what the outcome was, and any insight or lesson you gained
- Actively reflect during situations, so that you self-direct or self-correct and make changes to your behavior or words that bring about a more desirable outcome
- Reflect with others to gain an appreciation for their perspective and to broaden your awareness
- Maintain a high degree of awareness of the people, actions, interactions, and dynamics around you, in order to make sense of unknown, unexpected, or recognized situations as they occur
- Pay attention to the present moment; watch your thoughts with detachment and without judgment.

Potential Developmental Actions

Review the following ideas and tips to improve your effectiveness at active reflection in order to learn from experience. Identify one or two actions that you will work to integrate into your day-to-day work life.

Take The Time to Reflect On and Think About Situations You Have Been In At Work, What Your Behavior Was, How You Were Feeling, What The Outcome Was, and Any Insight or Lesson You Gained:

- **Be Intentional**
  - The difference between being intentional and unintentional about your own learning from experience is significant. When you are intentional about learning from experience and you have made learning one of your central goals, you are likely to examine your assumptions, methods, actions, and interpersonal relationships at every opportunity. When you are unintentional you sleepwalk through experiences without examining your assumptions, work methods, thinking processes, actions, or interpersonal relationships. Being intentional about your own learning from experience goes hand in hand with self-awareness; if you are intentional, you pay attention to yourself, to your own actions, to the reactions people have to you, and to the outcomes you produce.
  - To become more intentional about using reflection as a learning tool, *design reflection into your work* and identify opportunities to practice the skills you want to develop. *In the morning* take just a couple of minutes to think about the day ahead and consider questions such as:
    - Given my performance and development goals for the year, what are my highest priorities today?
    - Considering my development goals, what is one thing I can practice today?
    - What do I want to do "better" today? What will I do to accomplish that?
  - *At the end of the day* take time to reflect on what you experienced, to identify unexpected successes and failures, and think about any patterns that emerge in how you are leading.

- What went well? What didn't work well? Why?
- Looking back on your day, how closely did your actual results match what you expected? What were your unexpected successes? What were your unexpected failures? Are there any underlying patterns?
- How can you apply what you learned today to your work tomorrow?

  o Another way to be intentional about reflection and learning from experience is to **build milestones into your projects** at the conclusion of each phase of work to analyze what is working well, what isn't working, and what you want to improve going forward. Consider the following areas for potentially useful reflection as you review progress against your goals:
    - Roles and role clarity
    - Goals and goal clarity
    - Action planning
    - Decisions and decision making
    - Obstacles/barriers and how they were addressed
    - Recognition of team members' contributions
    - Values

- **Hit "Replay"**
  o As you reflect about a specific event or situation, replay the action as if you are watching a movie. It might help to close your eyes to visualize yourself in a specific situation. In your mind, go back to the beginning of the "scene" you want to reflect on, and picture yourself and others who were involved. Slowly let the scene unfold, and pay attention to what was said and done, how you and others reacted to what was said and done; watch closely to identify the interactions between yourself and others. As you "watch the movie," ask yourself these questions:
    - What took place?
    - What kind of impact did you have on others in the situation?

- What impact did they have on you?
- What new understanding did you develop about yourself, a colleague, or an aspect of the situation?

- **What? So What? Now What?**
  - Reflection can be as simple as asking yourself "What? So What? Now What?" This reflective technique guides you through a 3-step process designed to quickly and easily surface the essential elements of an experience and enables you to unearth meaning that otherwise might have gone unnoticed. It will be helpful to take notes about your reflection, so you can recall what took place in the experience and what you learned from it.
    - **What?** What happened during the interaction/situation? Try to recall as much of the interaction as possible, so you have maximum information available to work with as you reflect. If you made the call with a colleague or your manager, involve them in this reflection process as well; the different perspectives can be very valuable in recreating a vivid picture of what actually happened during the call. Typical questions asked in this stage include:
      - What did you just do?
      - What happened first, next, or last?
      - What did you intend to do?
      - What did you observe?
    - **So What?** With a clear description of the experience, ask some "So what?" questions. These questions engage you in critical thinking about the impact and consequences of their own actions. This is how you begin the process of transforming experience into knowledge. Some examples of "So What?" questions include:
      - What was good about what happened?
      - What could have been better?
      - How does this apply to you specifically?

- How was that significant?

- What struck you about that?

- What do you understand better about yourself or the team?

- **Now What?** Now you'll need to use your imagination, by taking the lessons learned from the experience and reapplying them to other situations. The questions are directed toward helping you apply the general knowledge they gained from the reflection so far, and applying them specifically to their own situations. Some examples of "Now What?" questions are:

  - What will you do again?

  - What will you do differently next time?

  - When, where, or how will you take different action?

  - What would you like to do with that information?

  - How could you repeat that experience?

- **Deeper Reflection: Double-Loop Learning**

  - The pace and complexity of modern business life often drives us to pursue an unending series of actions that we hope will produce the results we want to achieve, and never stopping to reflect. If we reflect on our experiences and actions at all, we may not go very deep, due to a need to move on to the next pressing priority. This tendency to just skim the surface of things, rather than considering deeper patterns of behavior, relationships between seemingly disconnected causes ("remote signals"), or dynamics of action and reaction is likely to yield limited insights into important patterns and trends embedded in our behavior. We need to practice "deep reflection," reflection that goes beyond the superficial and easily observed actions and results, and dives into the causes, motives, and patterns of our thinking and problem solving.

  - In his classic article "Teaching Smart People How to Learn" noted professor and author Chris Argyris wrote that leaders must "reflect critically on their own behavior, identify the ways they often inadvertently contribute to the organization's problems, and then change how they act. In particular, they must learn how the very way they go about defining and solving problems can be a source of problems in its own right" (Argyris, C. (1991). Teaching Smart People How to Learn. *Harvard Business Review, 69*(3), 99). Argyris distinguishes between what he called "double-loop" and "single-loop learning."

- *"Single-loop learning* is present when goals, values, frameworks, and, to a significant extent, strategies are taken for granted. The emphasis is on techniques and making techniques more efficient. Any reflection is directed toward making the strategy more effective. Essentially, if a specific action taken does not produce the results or consequences desired, the individual may reflect on the actions taken and decide what—if anything—he or she should do differently to achieve the desired results. *Double-loop learning* is required to address the deeper issues. At the root of double-loop learning is the idea that, to learn from experience, one must look deeper than one's actions; one must reflect on and evaluate one's values, beliefs, and "governing variables" to determine how one is contributing to a continuing pattern of behavior that does not result in what is wanted." (Argyris, C. 1991.)

- The following diagram illustrates the difference between single-loop and double-loop learning:

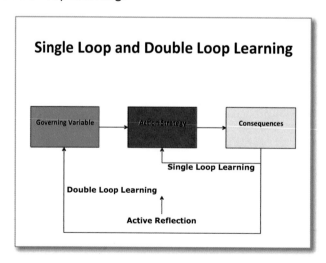

- Single-loop learning is present when goals, values, frameworks and, to a significant extent, strategies are taken for granted. The emphasis is on techniques and making techniques more efficient. Any reflection is directed toward making the strategy more effective. Essentially, if a specific action taken does not produce the results or consequences desired, the individual may reflect on the actions taken, and decide what – if anything – they should do differently to achieve the results they want.

- According to Argyris, single loop learning is driven by four "basic values:"

  - To remain in unilateral control

  - To maximize "winning" and to minimize "losing"

  - To suppress negative feelings

  - To appear as rational as possible

- Taken together, these values portray a profoundly defensive posture: a need to avoid embarrassment, threat, or feelings of vulnerability and incompetence. This **closed-loop reasoning explains why the mere encouragement of open inquiry can be intimidating to some**. And it's especially relevant to the behavior of many of the most highly skilled and best-trained employees. Behind their high aspirations are an equally high fear of failure and a tendency to be ashamed when they don't live up to their high standards. Consequently, they become brittle and despondent in situations in which they don't excel immediately. Learning from experience requires that we acknowledge that we have undoubtedly held to some or all of these values, consciously or not, and strive to avoid letting them continue to drive our behavior.

- Double loop learning sounds and looks more complicated than it really is. At its root, it is a very simple idea: To learn from experience, you have to look deeper than just your actions; you have to reflect on and evaluate your values, beliefs, and "governing variables" – your personal drivers – to see how you are contributing to a continuing pattern of behavior that doesn't get you what you want. Double-loop learning goes deeper than single loop learning, and involves questioning the governing variable – goals, values, and beliefs – that underlie explicit goals and strategies, and that drive behavior. Reflection here is more fundamental: the basic assumptions behind ideas or policies are confronted, or hypotheses are publicly tested. It's also not enough to reflect and evaluate these things privately, although that's part of it. It also requires interaction with others who are involved in the problem or situation.

Guided Practice: Reflection Using Double Loop Learning*

Context of Exercise: This is an exercise for self-reflection and learning. This method is particularly useful in situations where you experienced less than desirable results from your leadership intervention or strategy.

Exercise Steps: Individual Reflection

Identify a recent leadership experience that you had in which you had mixed results in terms of your outcomes.

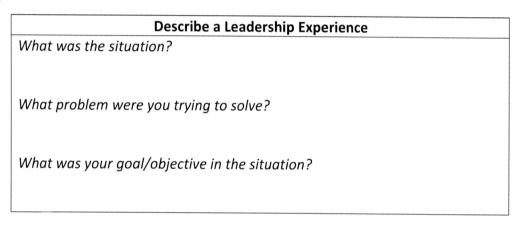

Describe a Leadership Experience
What was the situation?
What problem were you trying to solve?
What was your goal/objective in the situation?

Briefly, what stands out to you about what happened in this situation?

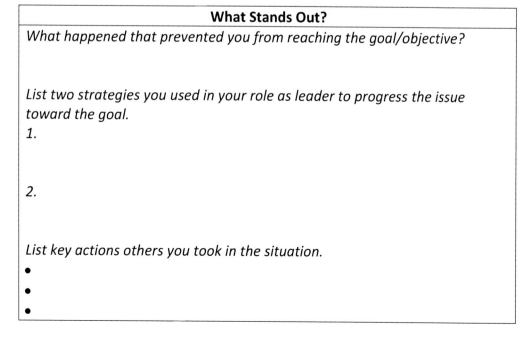

What Stands Out?
What happened that prevented you from reaching the goal/objective?
List two strategies you used in your role as leader to progress the issue toward the goal. *1.* *2.*
List key actions others you took in the situation. • • •

Select one of the strategies and make a brief note about two outcomes/consequences. List an outcome or consequence that you planned for and achieved and one that was unexpected or problematic.

Planned for & Achieved	Unexpected or Problematic

What is/was the underlying belief ("governing variable") you held about the issue or your approach to it that informed your choice of strategy?

The belief I held that informed my choice of strategy was:

How has acting on this belief created the two types of outcomes/consequences?

Achieving desired outcomes	Creating a new problem

Leadership Insights

- After some time reflecting, consider some other belief/s that might be more useful and appropriate in the future for progressing such issues. These beliefs might be about your role, style, approach to implementation, or about other people.

Alternate belief/s that might be more useful and appropriate:

Given the new insights into your beliefs, list one or two new/alternate strategies that might have the capacity to deliver different and positive outcomes while progressing your issue.

New/alternate strategies that might deliver better outcomes:

ACTIVELY REFLECT DURING SITUATIONS, SO THAT YOU SELF-DIRECT OR SELF-CORRECT AND MAKE CHANGES TO YOUR BEHAVIOR OR WORDS THAT BRING ABOUT A MORE DESIRABLE OUTCOME:

- **Look for Learning Opportunities**
    - Look for ways in which you can make learning a natural part of the job. Use daily problems to engage in double-loop learning; that is, not only solving the immediate problem but also figuring out how you can approach future problems more effectively.
    - Identify your personal barriers to learning. What tends to get in your way? Make a list of your personal learning preferences, and then make a list of your personal learning aversions, or types of learning you don't prefer. Remember that if you always stay inside your comfort zone, you limit what you can learn.
- **Keep It Simple**
    - Find ways to make reflection a natural part of your day. If you work in a structured selling organization that uses specific techniques and steps in a sales process, mentally add a step at the end of each sales call to reflect on the call. It can be as simple as asking

yourself "What? So What? Now What?" And it will be helpful to take notes about your reflection, so you can recall what took place in the experience and what you learned from it.

- **What?** What happened during the sales call? Try to recall as much of the interaction as possible, so you have maximum information available to work with as you reflect. If you made the call with a colleague or your manager, involve them in this reflection process as well; the different perspectives can be very valuable in recreating a vivid picture of what actually happened during the call. Typical questions asked in this stage include:
    - What did you just do?
    - What happened first, next, or last?
    - What did you intend to do?
    - What did you observe?

- **So What?** With a clear description of the experience, ask some "So what?" questions. These questions engage you in critical thinking about the impact and consequences of their own actions. This is how you begin the process of transforming experience into knowledge. Some examples of "So What?" questions include:
    - What was good about what happened?
    - What could have been better?
    - How does this apply to you specifically?
    - How was that significant?
    - What struck you about that?
    - What do you understand better about yourself or the team?

- **Now What?** Now you'll need to use your imagination, by taking the lessons learned from the experience and reapplying them to other situations. The questions are directed toward helping you apply the general knowledge they gained from the reflection so far, and applying them specifically to their own situations. Some examples of "Now What?" questions are:

- What will you do again?
- What will you do differently next time?
- When, where, or how will you take different action?
- What would you like to do with that information?
- How could you repeat that experience?

REFLECT WITH OTHERS TO GAIN AN APPRECIATION FOR THEIR PERSPECTIVE AND TO BROADEN YOUR AWARENESS:

- **Reflect With Others**
  - The Center for Creative Leadership describes how teams can reflect collectively in their Ideas Into Action Guidebook titled "<u>Critical Reflections: How Groups Can Learn from Success and Failure</u>" by Chris Ernst and André Martin. As people work together over time, certain key events stand out as having the potential to teach lasting lessons for the future. Leaders can use the Critical Reflections process to help their teams learn these lessons, whether the key event was a great success or a disappointing failure. The goal of this type of reflection is to help the team understand what happened so they can either repeat the success or to avoid repeating the same mistake. To use this approach of team reflection, follow these guidelines:
    - Before calling your group together for the Critical Reflections process, identify the key event (positive or negative), allocate time and space for the process, and prepare to orient your group.
    - The basic process includes three stages: exploring, reflecting, and projecting.
      - ***Exploring:*** In this stage the goal is to allow your team members to relive the event—to share perceptions, to appreciate differences, to identify overlaps and disconnects of personal experiences.
      - ***Reflecting:*** The reflecting stage provides the opportunity to interpret the event. How was it possible for the event to happen, and why did it?

- *Projecting:* Based on the group's understanding of what happened and how and why it happened, move into the projecting stage. Questions that are important to this stage of the process include:
  - What lessons can be learned?
  - What should team members keep doing, what should they stop doing, and what should they do differently?
  - What do they need to do either to repeat the current success or to avoid making the same mistake again?

- **Conduct After-Action Reviews**
  - After-Action Reviews (AAR) can be useful tools for group reflection. They can help a team identify what accounted for their success or failure, generate significant learning for a team, and articulate actions the team should consider taking in the future. AARs consist of a clear comparison of intended vs. actual actions planned and results achieved, and participants take learning from the review forward for application. One strong advantage of the AAR is that it can be conducted very quickly; to get the most from an After-Action Review (AAR), conduct it as soon after an experience or event as possible. Don't wait until the end of a project or the annual performance review.
  - Make sure that everyone who participated in the event or experience is present and participates; establish some ground rules – and follow them – to ensure that everyone feels comfortable sharing their perspective. If someone doesn't actively participate, invite their participation by saying something like, "John/Jane, you haven't had much to say so far. What's your take on this?"
  - There are three basic steps to an effective AAR:
    - **What was intended?** Describe what was planned or intended to occur in the experience or event being reviewed. This can include goals/objectives, activities/actions, and desired outcomes.

- **What actually happened?** Describe what actually happened during the experience. Did the team achieve the goals/objectives? Did the team take the actions that were planned? Were the desired outcomes reached?
    - Try to create an accurate picture of the experience you just completed. Capture what really occurred, like a video camera would record. This helps you identify and separate out the biases that prevent an accurate reconstruction of the experience.
    - Consider taking notes on a flip chart or white board so the whole group can see the picture of the experience. Encourage team members to take the marker and add to the picture or verbal description themselves.
    - All team members should have an active role in the discussion; make sure you hear from everyone, even those who do not normally speak up during meetings. The value in this activity is gaining the perspective and input from the diversity of the team.
- **What went well and why?** Identify actions/activities that went well, and the team's perspective on why those actions/activities went well (e.g., according to plan, achieved the desired objectives, etc.)
- **What can be improved and how?** Identify insights, feedback, and how the lessons of this experience can be applied to improve performance in the future.

MAINTAIN A HIGH DEGREE OF AWARENESS OF THE PEOPLE, ACTIONS, INTERACTIONS, AND DYNAMICS AROUND YOU, IN ORDER TO MAKE SENSE OF UNKNOWN, UNEXPECTED, OR RECOGNIZED SITUATIONS AS THEY OCCUR.

PAY ATTENTION TO THE PRESENT MOMENT; WATCH YOUR THOUGHTS WITH DETACHMENT AND WITHOUT JUDGMENT.

- **Practice Mindfulness**
    - Maintaining a high degree of awareness of the people and dynamics around you can be significantly enhanced if you practice "mindful awareness" or mindfulness. According to

the UCLA Mindful Awareness Research Center mindful awareness can be defined as "paying attention to present moment experiences with openness, curiosity and a willingness to be with what is. It is an excellent antidote to the stresses of modern times. It invites us to stop, breathe, observe, and connect with one's inner experience" (http://marc.ucla.edu, accessed Feb. 12, 2014). The practice of mindful awareness, or mindfulness, is credited with contributing to lower blood pressure, increasing attention and focus, relieving anxiety and depression, enhancing emotional well-being and lowering emotional reactivity, and strengthening decision making, emotional flexibility, and empathy. Mindful awareness enables us to practice active reflection *during* our lived experiences, which allows us to self-direct or self-correct more effectively.

o Much of the mindful awareness, or mindfulness, tools and resources available focus on certain practices that are designed to help us become more aware of simple things we can control, such as breathing, or our thoughts. As such, these practices tend to fall into the category of "meditation." For some, this implies that the practice of mindful awareness is "new age" hocus-pocus, and not something a serious-minded businessperson would or should be involved in. It brings to mind images of sitting cross-legged on the floor in yoga clothes, eyes closed and chanting "Ommmm." While many people do pursue mindfulness through yoga and other disciplines, the practice of mindful awareness takes many forms and can be easily implemented in the lives of busy executives through a few relatively simple techniques that don't involve actual meditation, chanting, or related activities that would look and feel out of place in an office setting.

o According to Forbes magazine "Mindfulness essentially means moment-to-moment awareness. Although it originated in the Buddhist tradition, you don't have to be Buddhist to reap its benefits". In his article "A Guide to Mindfulness at Work," Drew Hansen describes the basic philosophy of mindfulness this way: "When you are mindful...You become keenly aware of yourself and your surroundings, but you simply observe these things as they are. You are aware of your own thoughts and feelings, but you do not react to them in the way that you would if you were on "autopilot"…By not labeling or judging the events and circumstances taking place around you, you are freed from your normal tendency to react to them."

o The video from the TV show "60 Minutes," by Anderson Cooper illustrates how mindfulness can have a significant positive impact on awareness. "The newly mindful Anderson Cooper" can be found at https://youtu.be/vBhimxmhCpl .

o **Video Reflection**
- What did you see in the video that hit home with you?
- Can you identify any benefits to you or your team from becoming more mindful at work? At home?
- How could being more mindful help you with self-awareness and greater awareness of situations and people around you?

o Review the following tools and resources to enhance your ability to be focused and aware in the middle of the high-speed chaos of your everyday work life:
- Lifehack Presents: The Mindfulness Meditation Mini Guide (http://www.lifehack.org/articles/lifestyle/lifehack-presents-the-mindfulness-meditation-mini-guide.html) This is an extremely practical, business user-friendly website that explains what mindfulness is and is not, the benefits of mindfulness, and gives tips to getting started. Highly recommended.
- The Guided Meditation Site (http://www.the-guided-meditation-site.com/mindfulness.html) This website gives an introduction to mindfulness, the importance of switching off your "autopilot," some of the benefits of mindfulness, and recommends specific practices and techniques to improve your ability to maintain mindful awareness throughout your life.
- The Mindfulness Guide for the Super Busy: How to Live Life to the Fullest (http://zenhabits.net/the-mindfulness-guide-for-the-super-busy-how-to-live-life-

to-the-fullest/) This blog post recommends practical steps on "How to Be Mindful."

- The *quite* short guide to mindfulness (http://www.padraigomorain.com/the-quite-short-guide-to-mindfulness.html) This is a highly practical, simple, one-page guide on how to begin practicing mindfulness, and is perfect for busy people.

- **Start Making Sense!**
  - ○ "Sensemaking, a term introduced by Karl Weick, refers to how we structure the unknown so as to be able to act in it. Sensemaking involves coming up with a plausible understanding—a map—of a shifting world; testing this map with others through data collection, action, and conversation; and then refining, or abandoning, the map depending on how credible it is . . . . Sensemaking can be broken down into three core elements: exploring the wider system, creating a map of the current situation, and acting to change the system to learn more about it" (Ancona, 2012). The steps involved in each of these three core elements are listed below, and a link to an article describing this process in more detail is provided at the end of this section.

    - ▪ *Exploring the Wider System*
      1. Seek out many types and sources of data. Combine financial data with trips to the shop floor, listen to employees as well as customers, and mix computer research with personal interviews.
      2. Involve others as you try to make sense of any situation. Your own mental model of what is going on can only get better as it is tested and modified through interaction with others.
      3. Move beyond stereotypes. Rather than oversimplifying – "Marketing people are always overestimating the demand" – try to understand the nuances of each particular situation.

4. Be very sensitive to operations. Learn from those closest to the front line, to customers, and to new technologies. What trends do current shifts portend for the future? What's behind the trends that we see recurring in different parts of the world?

- ***Creating a Map of the Current Situation***

    5. Do not simply overlay your existing framework on a new situation. The new situation may be very different. Instead, let the appropriate map or framework emerge from your understanding of the situation.

    6. Put the emerging situation into a new framework to provide organizational members with order. Use images, metaphors, and stories to capture key elements of the new situation.

- ***Acting to Change the System to Learn From It***

    7. Learn from small experiments. If you are not sure how a system is working, try something new.

    8. People create their own environments and are then constrained by them. Be aware and realize the impact of your own behavior in creating the environment in which you are working.

Source: The Handbook for Teaching Leadership. (2012, Sage Publications) Chapter 1: Sensemaking: Framing and Acting in the Unknown, by Deborah Ancona. (http://www.sagepub.com/upm-data/42924_1.pdf)

"If you want to be a good global leader, you have to have a degree of openness and self-reflection. And you have to have a humbleness, of saying that you don't know it all, and you're willing to learn and you're willing to rely on others. And that's an uncomfortable feeling for a lot of people."

Global Leader, in How Global Leaders Develop, 2010

- **Keep a Learning Journal**
  - Many people use a learning journal to increase their awareness of daily events and the learning opportunities that occur. Like many of the Learning Practices described in this guide, keeping a Learning Journal requires self-discipline, structure, and organization. The next section of the guide provides an outline of how to set up and use a learning journal as a tool for reflection and development.

Learning Journal

Purpose

The purpose of a Learning Journal is to enable you to maximize your learning from experience. You do this by capturing your first-hand experiences in your own words in your learning journal, reflecting on those experiences and words, developing new insights and learning from your reflective observation, and applying those insights and learning – with an honest desire to grow, develop, and change – in new situations to enhance your effectiveness.

Using a Learning Journal

1. **What is a learning journal?**

   - A learning journal is a document that you (the learner) write to record the progress of your learning and development. You use your learning journal to capture your observations, insights, questions, and challenges.

   - However, it is used not only to record experiences and events over a period of time. It also entails conscious reflection and commentary. A learning journal is most useful when you – the learner – and review and reflect on what you have written.

2. **How do you write a learning journal?**

   - Pay particular attention to situations that are related to the actions on your Individual Development Plan. Every time you write in your journal, try to write something related to your IDP. For example, write about how you saw your strength in action, and what it did for you. Write about what action you took while working to improve on a development opportunity.

   - A learning journal is not the "great American novel." It doesn't have to be refined, use proper grammar, spelling, etc. It is a highly personal reflection on your own experience – your actions, observations, feelings, questions, insights, worries, accomplishments, and even your let-downs or failures.

- A basic framework for starting a learning journal is to use these four basic elements, developed by David Kolb and discussed in his book <u>Experiential Learning: Experience as the Source of Learning and Development</u>[12]:

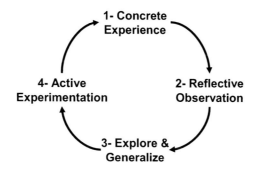

1. **Concrete Experience** – Write a **description** of the situation/experience, including what you did, what others did, their reactions, your reactions, the impact of your actions, and your feelings at the time

2. **Reflective Observation** – **Reflect** on the situation/experience you wrote about. Given some distance and time to reflect, do you see that situation any differently? If so, how? What new insights can you identify? Do you see any patterns in your behavior?

3. **Explore & Generalize** – Given your reflection, consider how these observations might apply to the way you lead in other circumstances, and think about how you can **generalize** what you have learned. Do you see any parallels to other situations or people? What can you do to use your insights to enhance your effectiveness as a leader

4. **Active Experimentation** – **Apply** your insights in new situations, and **actively experiment** with new behaviors or actions. These then become the subject of future journal entries.

3. **What form should your journal take?**

- Use a form that you are most comfortable with personally.

- Notebooks and binders of loose-leaf paper allow you to quickly and easily jot notes to yourself and store them for easy access. The loose-leaf journal can be reorganized, but can also more easily lose pages. The notebook journal is less flexible, but may feel more permanent.

---

[12] Experiential Learning: Experience as the Source of Learning and Development. Pearson Education, 2015.

- We highly recommend that you keep your journal in a notebook and write your entries by hand, rather than on a computer. However, if you find it significantly easier to write at a computer keyboard, by all means use your computer. You can print out the pages and keep them in a loose-leaf binder. Some people prefer to use a computer software program to keep their journal, and never print it. One advantage of keeping a learning journal on your computer is that you can easily search and reorganize your journal entries.

4. **How much time should you spend on the learning journal? How much should you write?**

- Try to find a regular, convenient time where you can have 10-15 minutes of time to reflect on your experience at work.

- To make the journal process work for you, you will probably need to write in your journal at least weekly.

- If you're writing just a sentence or two each time you write in your journal, that's probably not enough to truly take advantage of the journal process. But, there is no magic number of words or paragraphs; you will have to find your own comfort level. One guideline is to write at least one paragraph of at least 4 – 5 sentences related to the items on your IDP, every time you sit down to write in your journal.

5. **Use these questions to get started in your learning journal.**

- As I look back on the day/week, what were the most significant events or interactions?

- Did I have any particularly meaningful conversations?

- Did I do any reading? What were my reactions to it?

- How did I feel during the day/week? What were the emotional highs and lows? Why did I feel as I did?

- Did I find myself worrying about anything today/this week?

- What did I accomplish on the job today/this week?

- What did I accomplish in relation to my IDP today/this week?

- Did I fail at anything? Struggle at anything? What can I learn from this?

- What did I learn today/this week?

- When did I feel the most engaged, excited, stimulated?

- What could I do to become more effective and satisfied in my role?

6. How can you learn from your journal?

- Make regular entries over time

- Periodically review and read your journal entries, and reflect on what you read.

- Write new journal entries that explore your journal reflections.

- Ask yourself:

  - Are there experiences, situations, or understandings that stand out for me? What is it about them that catches my attention?
  - Does what I wrote in my journal still seem right to me? Have I been completely honest? Do the interpretations of events I made at the time still stand up?
  - What is missing? Have I evaded anything, or not been completely honest with myself about anything?
  - Do I see any patterns of behavior over time that I am pleased about? Concerned about?

Learning Journal: Example

Introduction

Getting started with keeping a personal learning journal is often the most difficult part. Somehow, just making that first entry on the blank page or screen is intimidating. The beauty of the learning journal is that, no matter <u>what</u> you write, or <u>how well</u> (or poorly) you write, as long as you take the time to write down your thoughts and reflections about your experience…you can't be wrong!

This example of an initial entry in a personal learning journal may help you understand how easy it is to get started.

Date:	January 15

OK….well, this is my first entry in my personal learning journal, and I'm not really sure what I'm supposed to write about. I'm not really a great writer or anything, and I don't know exactly what I'm supposed to get out of doing this either. But, I'm willing to give it a try. It seems simple enough. My plan is to take one hour on Friday morning, at the beginning of the day, and think back over what happened during the week.
For now, I think I'll be focusing on the #1 development need on my IDP: Competency #34 – "Holds frequent discussions to guide development; Identifies strengths and skill improvement opportunities, and provides timely, constructive feedback and coaching." It came through pretty clearly as the #1…basically, it was a

strong theme that I saw throughout all my feedback sources: my Hogan feedback report, my last Performance Evaluation, my Leadership Competency Self-Assessment, AND my manager's assessment of me.

So, I have a draft of my IDP, and I'm going to talk to Fred (my manager) about that next week. I think it's pretty good, but I could use some ideas on, and definitely want to get Fred's support for what I'm planning to do. I actually tried something different yesterday, that I guess falls into the "low-hanging fruit" category: I ordered a book I found recommended in the Developmental Resource Guide on how to give feedback and coaching. It looked pretty good, and had good reviews online.

I also sat down with my direct reports last week and told them that I had just done the Leadership Competency Assessment process, and had identified a strength to leverage and 3 development needs to improve on. It felt kind of awkward to tell <u>them</u> about my strength and development opportunities, and it seemed like they didn't know what to do about it. But once I did it, I was glad, because they were pretty supportive, and said they would try to help me however they could. They also wanted to know if they could use an assessment and development process for themselves! That was pretty cool!

So, it looks like I've written almost a page here, and I'm running out of time. This wasn't as hard as I thought it might be, so I guess I'll be back with more entries next week.

Learning Journal Framework - Example

A basic framework for starting a learning journal is to use these four basic elements as the structure for your journal entries:

1. **Concrete Experience** – Write a **description** of the situation/experience, including what you did, what others did, their reactions, your reactions, the impact of your actions, and your feelings at the time.
I met with my direct reports to tell them that I had completed the Leadership Competency Assessment process, and that it was very helpful. I told them what I identified as my strength to leverage, and the 3 developmental opportunities I identified. They seemed kind of curious, like they weren't sure of what to expect, and surprised that I told them these things. I felt a little awkward at first, but it seemed to work out ok. They were supportive and said they would do whatever they could to help me out. They also wanted to know if they could do something similar! So now we're going to talk about them next week.
2. **Reflective Observation** – **Reflect** on the situation/experience you wrote about. Given some distance and time to reflect, do you see that situation any differently? If so, how? What new insights can you identify? Do you see any patterns in your behavior?

I think they could probably sense my awkward feelings in that meeting. But it was an awkward thing: I felt like I was telling them that I had not been a very good manager, since I need to work on Feedback and Coaching. I suppose I don't want to look bad in front of them, so I try to keep up an appearance. Thing is, they already knew anyway, since they're the ones I'm supposed to be coaching. I think I also need to work on being more open, with less of a blind spot, and get more comfortable about admitting when I need help.

3. **Generalization** – Given your reflection, consider how these observations might apply to the way you lead in other circumstances, and think about how you can **generalize** what you have learned. Do you see any parallels to other situations or people? What can you do to use your insights to enhance your effectiveness as a leader.

Now that I think about it, this same thing happens at home, with my spouse... It's just hard to be open and honest about things that I think I should be doing better. But, the reaction I got from my directs was pretty positive, and my spouse is pretty positive and supportive, too. I think I have to figure out how to get over that fear.

4. **Active Experimentation** – **Apply** your insights in new situations, and **actively experiment** with new behaviors or actions. These then become the subject of future journal entries.

I think I'll try to be more open and honest about my own development needs, and try to ask for more help. I don't think I'll go crazy asking everybody about every little thing, but it probably wouldn't hurt to ask for help every now and then. I'll have a chance to talk to my manager about this next week, so that's how I'll try to apply this.

Self-Assessment: Score Yourself on Active Reflection / Mindfulness

Think about your work and life experiences over the past year and answer the following questions using this scale:

Never (1)   Rarely (2)   Sometimes (3)   Often (4)   Almost always (5)

- I take the time to reflect on and think about situations I have been in at work, what my behavior was, how I was feeling, what the outcome was, and any insight or lesson I gained.   **1   2   3   4   5**

- I actively reflect during situations, so that I self-direct or self-correct and make changes to my behavior or words that bring about a more desirable outcome.   **1   2   3   4   5**

- I reflect with others to gain an appreciation for their perspective and to broaden my awareness.   **1   2   3   4   5**

- I maintain a high degree of awareness of the people, actions, interactions, and dynamics around me, in order to make sense of situations and experiences as they occur.   **1   2   3   4   5**

- Pay attention to the present moment; watch your thoughts with detachment and without judgment.   **1   2   3   4   5**

OVERALL SCORE:
Sum of Ratings divided by 4 (Number of Items)

Guide to Interpreting Your Overall Score

- If your overall score on this learning practice is 15 or less, it may be time to examine your skills of reflection and situational awareness. How much energy and time do you invest in reflection in order to learn from experiences? What can you do to intentionally reflect on experience? Refer to the Potential Developmental Actions for ideas on how you can more effectively integrate this Learning Practice into your work life.

- If your overall score on this learning practice is 16 to 19, you are already utilizing reflection and situational awareness as a tool to learn from experience. By increasing your use of these practices you can learn even more, more quickly from your experiences. Think about ways you can begin to reflect on your experience more frequently. Review the Potential Developmental Actions for ideas on how you can integrate reflection and situational awareness into your daily work life.

- If your overall score on this learning practice is 20 or above, congratulations! Active Reflection and Situational Awareness can easily erode or fade away without constant attention and practice. Teaching others how to use this learning practice can help you stay sharp. Keep it up!

REFLECTION QUESTIONS

What challenges to actively reflecting, if any, do you experience in your job?

What impact has active reflection had on your learning, growth, and development as a leader?

Think about a situation in which you intentionally used reflection on experience to contribute to your learning, growth, and development as a leader. What was the situation? How did you use reflection? What did you learn? What changes did you make as a result?

How frequently do you use reflection as a development tool? How could you use reflection more frequently?

How do you coach and mentor others to use active reflection to assist in their growth and development?

How do you practice mindfulness in your work and life? What can you do maintain a mindful approach to work?

9. Actively Experiment With New Approaches

"I have experimented with adapting new leadership styles when I'm having difficulty leading, influencing and coaching an employee who isn't showing growth or change. This comes from the thought that it's often easier for me to adapt my own leadership style to the employee rather than the employee adapting to me. This has helped me achieve different, better and faster outcomes when leading, coaching and managing employee performance."

Rick Ramos, PerkinElmer

Introduction

Learning and developing from experience is enhanced when you actively experiment with new approaches based on your analysis of prior experience, try out new behaviors, employ trial and error and active experimentation in decision making and problem solving, and analyze your mistakes as sources of learning. Leaders who use these learning strategies gain more from their experience.

In my research[13] into how global leaders develop I discovered that they learned through many different means. They learned intuitively, in an unplanned and unstructured manner. They learned through observation of people and the organizations they worked in; by seeking and accepting feedback from others; from their own mistakes and failures; from active experimentation, reflection-in-action, and other ad hoc learning tactics.

If you are in a leadership position, you may already engage in a wide range of learning approaches or tactics that enhance your learning from experience. If not, try to utilize various approaches to evaluate what works best for you. The key descriptors of this continuous learning best practice and the suggestions on how to implement them may provide some help on "how to" Actively Experiment with New Approaches.

Review the list of behaviors, behavioral trends and patterns, and tendencies below. As you do, reflect on your own experience and try to recall specific situations or events that shed light on your own patterns of behavior related to this Learning Practice.

---

[13] *How Global Leaders Develop.* UMI/Proquest, 2010.

BEHAVIORS, BEHAVIORAL TRENDS AND PATTERNS, TENDENCIES:

- Frequently try different approaches to solving problems
- Play around with different ways of presenting an idea you have
- Brainstorm with colleagues new ways of doing what you have done for years

Potential Developmental Actions

Review the following for examples of developmental actions you can take to enhance your effectiveness at actively experimenting with new approaches to work and learning as a leader as you do. Identify at least one action that you will work to integrate into your day-to-day work life.

FREQUENTLY TRY DIFFERENT APPROACHES TO SOLVING PROBLEMS:

- Business challenges and problems seem to get more complex and difficult with each passing day. Change is constant and rapid, leading to a widespread perception that business conditions in the world are Volatile, Uncertain, Complex, and Ambiguous (VUCA). This puts pressure on us to be constantly at our mental best, able to anticipate and respond to change in the moment. However, most of us are creatures of habit, turning to familiar, "tried and true" approaches to solve new, unfamiliar problems. However, as Henry Ford once said, "If you always do what you've always done, you'll always get what you've always got." Recognizing that this is true is only the first step towards changing; doing something other than what you've always done is the challenge.

- Change is hard, no doubt about it. But you can change if you work at it in the right way. Leaders who consistently, rigorously, and intentionally use the Learning Practices learn, grow, and develop significantly more, faster while achieving better results. The key to this type of change is deliberate practice, informed by reflection, and anchored in reality by accountability.

- So, how can we break out of our old patterns of behavior and change for the better? We're going to review several concepts that will help you break out of the old habits that keep you from higher levels of performance. Bear in mind that they work best if you use them consistently, rigorously, and intentionally. These concepts are System 1/System 2 Thinking; Focus; and Design Thinking.

- **System 1/System 2 Thinking** are two distinct modes of thinking described by Daniel Kahneman in Thinking, Fast and Slow.[14] System 2 thinking is the controlled, logical type of thinking typical of rational management. It's slow, effortful, logical, calculating, and conscious and is a product of our "evolved mind." In addition to System 2 thinking from our evolved mind, we also have the "primitive brain" that provides us with System 1 thinking capabilities: fast, holistic, automatic, subconscious, intuitive, and emotional. It could even be described as "immediate cognition without thought."[15]

- To effectively confront the complex challenges of our VUCA world, and to break out of the old, familiar ways of thinking, we need to take advantage of these System 1 cognitive skills, and to do so we need to intentionally manage them. We're going to focus on a few key cognitive skills that all within System 1: Attentional Control, Metacognition, and Sensemaking.

- **Attentional Control**
    - Attentional Control is the conscious control of your own attention. You might also think of it as mindfulness, situational awareness, and focus. We live in a fast-paced, highly distracting world in which we are pulled in multiple directions at once. One of the biggest distractions in this VUCA world is our smartphones. The short video clip provided at the link below illustrates some of the side effects of a deficit in Attentional Control, or Situational Awareness.

---

[14] Thinking, Fast and Slow, Farrar, Straus and Giroux, 2011
[15] On Being Certain, St. Martin's Griffin, 2008, p. 138.

"Texting While Walking"

Our devices often rule our lives in uncomfortable ways. Parents are increasingly aware of the amount of "screen time" their children engage in, and yet leaders are subject to the lure of the screen as well. Watch this short video that illustrates some of the results of being distracted while texting, and then use the questions below to reflect.

YouTube Video: https://youtu.be/_cznepJAbyg

- **Video Reflection**
    - What were your thoughts upon viewing the video?
    - How were the individuals depicted functioning, or performing, while being distracted?
    - Did they demonstrate good attentional control or situational awareness?

    - Distractions are everywhere! If you can relate to this video or have been guilty of "Texting While Walking," you may need to work on increasing your Attentional Control, or Cognitive Shifting abilities. Cognitive shifting is the mental process of consciously redirecting one's attention away from one fixation to another. Strength in cognitive shifting allows you to take charge of your mental habits and redirect your focus in more helpful directions.
    - Mindfulness has emerged as an increasingly popular practice of self-management and is in a sense an antidote to Mindlessness or a failure of Attentional Control and lack of Focus. The video "The newly mindful Anderson Cooper", from the TV show "60 Minutes," illustrates how mindfulness can have a significant positive impact on Attentional Control. The video can be found at https://youtu.be/vBhimxmhCpI .

"The newly mindful Anderson Cooper"

- **Video Reflection**
    - What did you see in the video that hit home with you?
    - Can you identify any benefits to you or your team from becoming more mindful at work? At home?
    - How could being more mindful help you with solving problems?

- **Improving Attentional Control**
    - Improving your Attentional Control will require deliberate practice, reflection, and accountability for change. Making this change happen is difficult to accomplish on your own, so we recommend you work with a coach, a colleague, or even a therapist who is trained in this area. If you decide to work on this skill, or want to learn more about it before you make a decision, you may want to consult these resources to help with your planning and development:
        - How cognitive shifting principles apply to everyday life
            - <u>The Way of the Tiger</u>, by Lance Secretan
            - <u>The Creative Manager,</u> by Peter Russell
        - The process of conscious choosing and cognitive shifting, breaking out of old patterns in our lives
            - <u>The Courage to Create</u>, Rollo May, 1994
        - Consciously shifting from a negative to a more positive emotional focus
            - <u>The Emotional Brain</u>, Joseph LeDoux

- <u>**Metacognition**</u>
    - Metacognition is the awareness and control of your own mental and emotional processes; it's literally "thinking about your thinking." It is an element of self-awareness and can be strengthened through reflection and keeping a learning journal. Both

reflection and learning journals are addressed elsewhere in the Guide to Intentional Learning from Experience (click on the hyperlinks for content).

- **Sensemaking**
    - Sensemaking is the ability to quickly connect the dots to gain understanding. It is pattern-based reasoning; in other words, it's the process of developing an understanding of an event or situation, particularly if it's complex and you lack clear, complete, and orderly data. Good sense-makers "put the pieces together" quickly and effectively overcome gaps in information. They discern meaning from complex patterns and recognize how parts of a system fit into the bigger picture. This allows them to notice potential opportunities or problems before they become fully apparent.
    - You can begin developing your sensemaking skills by systematically exploring widely divergent points of view and information from a variety of sources.
        - **Make a reading list** of 10 journals or professional periodicals from 10 completely different disciplines, none of which you have previously subscribed to or read. Then develop a schedule to read each journal/periodical every month for a year. At the end of each month, reflect on what you read during the previous month and look for themes, trends, and connections among the publications. Use a learning journal to capture your thoughts and reflections. On a regular basis, share the new connections you have made with a colleague or friend. Describing the new insights and connection points you have made will help you get very clear about your thinking.
        - **Become a voracious consumer** of a wide array of media in addition to journals and professional periodicals. Make it a habit to reflect regularly to identify connections among these disparate information sources.
        - **Form a learning group** that focuses on group sensemaking through reading and other media. Meet with group members regularly to share and discuss the insights you have gained and questions you have developed as a result of your

broader intake of information. Use the group discussion to identify connections between the various readings and media you have jointly explored.

- o **"Weak Signals"** are also elements of sensemaking. Weak signals are snippets of information that are found in disparate streams of data that may not be recognized as valuable or meaningful, until someone identifies how they connect to bigger issues and articulates both how they connect as well as the implications.
    - The following articles provide an introduction to weak signals and their relevance for leaders in today's challenging environment.
        - *The strength of 'weak signals,'* by Martin Harrysson, Estelle Metayer, and Hugo Sarrazin, in McKinsey Quarterly, Feb. 2014. https://www.mckinsey.com/industries/high-tech/our-insights/the-strength-of-weak-signals
        - *The Skill of Reading Weak Signals in Leadership Situations*, by Robert Brodo, March 21, 2017. http://www.advantexe.com/blog/the-skill-of-reading-weak-signals-in-leadership-situations

PLAY AROUND WITH DIFFERENT WAYS OF PRESENTING AN IDEA YOU HAVE:

- No doubt we all have had our fill of slide presentations, with too many slides that have way too many words in font sizes that no one can possibly read, and delivered in an unenthusiastic manner and unexpressive voice. Who doesn't love listening to *that* in a stuffy conference room on a beautiful Friday afternoon?

- Changing the way you present ideas and information can be pretty daunting, especially if your attempt to be creative doesn't work out well or you go down in flames. Once burned, twice shy, as they say. However, this is one Learning Practice that really does require deliberate practice to produce results, and you won't get any better at presenting your ideas unless you actually present your ideas, learn from the experience, and change something about the way you present the next time.

- Here are a few ways to play around with different ways of presenting an idea you have:
    - **Mind-Mapping** can be used to help you learn effectively, improve the way you take notes, make your problem solving more creative, and presenting information in a format that illustrates the overall structure of your topic.
    - **Observe someone** whose presentations you admire, paying close attention to their presentation approach, methods, and tools. Take notes, and meet with them after the presentation to ask them how they go about preparing and delivering an effective presentation. The next time you have a presentation to make, apply what you learned from that person, and ask them to observe you, take notes, and share their feedback with you. Learning of this type is all about incremental change over time. You will probably need to make several presentations before you become comfortable using an approach that is significantly different from your standard, "go to" approach.
    - **Find a book on presentation skills** and adopt one or more of the recommendations that is different than your usual way of thinking or presenting. One book that you may find useful is The Presentation Secrets of Steve Jobs.[16] This book describes the specific techniques that made Jobs such a captivating presenter, and uses them as a blueprint to enable others to emulate his approach. Chances are you will pick up at least one "nugget" of gold to experiment with in your own presentations.
- **Learning from your experience** – No matter what new technique or approach you use to present an idea you have, be sure to plan ahead to make the most of the experience. Integrating a few simple steps into your experiment, trial and error, or practice session can make the difference between learning and merely wasted time. So, try this simple approach:
    - **Purposefully adopt a Learning Mindset** – To get the most out of this experiment, you will need to maintain mindful awareness of your own feelings and thoughts, and pay attention to how others respond to your presentation.

---

[16] The Presentation Secrets of Steve Jobs, Carmine Gallo. McGraw Hill, 2010.

- Reflect and Journal – As you go through this process, make a few notes in your Learning Journal to capture your thoughts and feelings, any insights you gain along the way, and how people respond to your new approach.

- Set a goal – Choose a specific skill, technique, or approach that you want to try out in your presentation, such as story-telling, or mind-mapping. Tell someone you trust that you are trying something new, and ask for their help and support by observing and giving you feedback. Write your goal in your Learning Journal.

- Prepare the presentation – Using the skill, technique, or approach you want to try out, prepare your presentation. Make notes in your Learning Journal about the preparation process, not about the steps to prepare but about your thoughts and feelings related to doing something different that may hold an element of risk.

- Deliver the presentation – Follow through on your presentation plan. As you deliver the presentation, maintain mindful awareness of yourself as you present. This is "self-observation," in which you try to step outside of yourself to observe yourself in action. Try to notice what you are doing, while you are doing it. This will give you greater flexibility and presence of mind during your presentation.

- Reflect – Before you talk to anyone else about the presentation, take the time to reflect and capture your thoughts in your Learning Journal, using these questions:
  - What did I do that went well?
  - What did I do that didn't do as well as I would have liked?
  - What will I do differently next time?

- Solicit feedback – After your presentation is done, ask your colleague(s) to share their observations. If you haven't already done so, share your goal with them and ask for feedback that is behavioral, detailed, and specific. Try not to get engaged in a debate or discussion, and avoid becoming defensive about what they tell you. Just say "thank you," make notes of what they say, and move on.

- Synthesize – Review your own notes and the feedback from your colleague, and identify any insights and themes. In your Learning Journal, capture your thoughts to the same questions listed above, but now with the benefit of hearing feedback from someone else. You might even now have a discussion with someone to share your own insights and learning, the feedback you received, and what you now believe you want to do to keep moving forward.

BRAINSTORM WITH COLLEAGUES NEW WAYS OF DOING WHAT YOU HAVE DONE FOR YEARS:

○ Brainstorming is a technique for generating lots of radical, creative ideas. It is often used to address difficult problems and solutions are not readily apparent. It can be very helpful in identifying new ways of tackling problems and generating buy-in from group members who participate in the brainstorming process.

○ "Brainstorming combines a relaxed, informal approach to problem solving with lateral thinking. It encourages people to come up with thoughts and ideas that can, at first, seem a bit crazy. Some of these ideas can be crafted into original, creative solutions to a problem while others can spark even more ideas. This helps to get people unstuck by "jolting" them out of their normal ways of thinking."[17]

○ One of the critical elements of effective brainstorming is that participants are expected to avoid criticizing or praising ideas, in order to open up possibilities and identify as many ideas as possible. Evaluating ideas during the idea generation phase of brainstorming only shuts down creative thinking instead of opening it up. The time to evaluate ideas is at the end of the brainstorming session, when the group is ready to consider likely solutions to pursue further.

○ Brainstorming can be an individual activity or a group activity, and there are pros and cons associated with both approaches, as illustrated in the table below.

---

[17] Brainstorming. MindTools, https://www.mindtools.com/brainstm.html

	Individual Brainstorming	Group Brainstorming
Pro	• Can produce more and better ideas than Group Brainstorming • Don't have to worry about ideas being evaluated or criticized during the process, so more ideas can be generated • Don't have to deal with group member behavior that can interfere with productivity • Can be most effective when trying to solve a simple problem or generate ideas	• Multiple perspectives from a diverse group can yield many valuable ideas • When one person gets stuck with an idea, other group members can advance the idea further • Can develop ideas further in group brainstorming • Contributes to buy-in to the solution because everyone had input • Can be a valuable team-building activity
Con	• You don't have the diverse perspectives and ideas of a group to stimulate thinking • You may not develop your ideas as fully on your own	• Some people may find the group setting to be stifling, so care must be taken to ensure everyone has a chance to contribute • Inappropriate group member behavior can potentially derail or limit the effectiveness of the brainstorming process

How to Run a Group Brainstorming Session[18]

1. **Prepare the Group**

   a. Find a comfortable location for the session, ensuring that you have the materials and resources you need

   b. Provide an appropriate amount of information to the group in advance to enable them to be ready when they walk in the room.

   c. Select the participants carefully, so that you have an appropriate mix of people who can add something to the session.

   d. Ask someone to be the timekeeper and someone else to be in charge of taking notes.

2. **Present the Problem**

   a. Familiarize the group with the Learning Mindset model, and the Learning Practices that seem most relevant to the session. Encourage them to engage in the session with a Learning Mindset, and to "practice the practices" to ensure a productive session.

   b. Lead a discussion with the group on some "operating principles" that everyone agrees to follow during the session. Typically, these are things such as: listen to

---

[18] Brainstorming. MindTools, https://www.mindtools.com/brainstm.html

understand; everyone actively participates but no one person dominates; engage in the session with an open mind; ask great questions; actively reflect; be mindfully aware and present in the session; etc.

c. Describe the problem to the group as clearly as you can, and communicate the desired outcome from the session.

d. To get things moving, start by having people write down their initial ideas and then share those ideas with the group.

3. Guide the Discussion

a. Be a role model of the Learning Mindset during the session, and encourage the group to use the session as an opportunity to learn from experience.

b. Ask group members which Learning Practices they want to use during the session, to improve their learning from experience.

c. Lead the group to the point where all their ideas have been shared. The group doesn't need to achieve deep understanding of ideas at this stage; it's more important to get the ideas in the room, and use them to identify more ideas.

d. After the group has finished generating ideas, facilitate a discussion that more fully develops the ideas and generates more ideas.

e. Encourage everyone to participate in the discussion, and carefully ensure that the more talkative members give enough air time and space for the less talkative ones.

f. Be sure to rely on the timekeeper for awareness of the schedule, and on the "scribe" to capture key ideas and decisions the group reaches.

g. As a conclusion of the Brainstorming session, ask the group members to reflect on the process and on their participation, and then share any insights or learning they gained. Ask them how they improved their ability to learn from experience.

h. After the Brainstorming session has concluded, be sure to take the time to reflect yourself, as the Facilitator.

    i. What worked well in the session?

    ii. What didn't work as well as you had hoped?

iii. How effective were you at enacting a Learning Mindset during the session, and at explaining the Learning Mindset to the group?

iv. How effectively did you utilize specific Learning Practices during the session to enhance your ability to learn from the experience?

v. What would you do differently next time?

- You can use brainstorming or some of the alternative techniques listed on the Mindtools website to identify new ways of doing what you have done in the past. Sometimes it's good just to shake things up and try new and different approaches to the old "tried and true" ways you have always done things. This may be even more true when these familiar approaches are no long producing the type of results needed in more current times. There may not be a need to change things up for the sake of change, but trying new approaches to old problems can also generate new energy and engagement in a team or organization!

- For additional ideas and techniques to improve your brainstorming sessions, refer to the Mindtools website on brainstorming. You may also find value in learning about an alternative to brainstorming called "Question-Storming" that is discussed elsewhere in this Guide.

"Negative results are just what I want. They're just as valuable to me as positive results. I can never find the thing that does the job best until I find the ones that don't."

Thomas A. Edison

Self-Assessment: Score Yourself on Actively Experimenting with New Approaches

Think about your work and life experiences over the past year and answer the following questions using this scale:

Never (1) Rarely (2) Sometimes (3) Often (4) Almost always (5)

- I frequently try different approaches to solving problems. **1 2 3 4 5**

- I play around with different ways of presenting an idea I have. **1 2 3 4 5**

- I brainstorm with colleagues new ways of doing what I have done for years. **1 2 3 4 5**

OVERALL SCORE:
Sum of Ratings divided by 3 (Number of Items)

Guide to Interpreting Your Overall Score

- If your overall score on this learning practice is 9 or less, think about how you approach solving problems and generating ideas. How can you experiment with new approaches to old problems? Refer to the Potential Developmental Actions for ideas on how you can more effectively integrate this Learning Practice into your work life.

- If your overall score on this learning practice is 10 to 14, you are already trying to experiment with different approaches. Think about ways you can more frequently try different approaches to solving problems and experimenting with different ways of presenting your ideas. Review the Potential Developmental Actions for ideas on how you can enhance your effectiveness at this learning practice into your daily work life.

- If your overall score on this learning practice is 18 or above, congratulations! Active experimentation with new approaches to solving problems and achieving results makes valuable contributions to learning from experience. Continue to rely on this learning practice as an important tool in your ongoing development as a leader.

REFLECTION QUESTIONS

What difficult problems does your organization face that could benefit from new or different approaches?

Think about a situation in which you tried a different approach to solving problems. What was the problem? How did you approach solving it? How was that approach different from a more "standard" approach? What was the outcome?

What is one concrete example of you brainstorming with colleagues to identify new ways of solving a problem or achieving a goal? Reflecting on that experience now, what did you learn? How did this experience impact how you approach problems or goals?

What have you done in the last year to actively experiment with new and different approaches to improve your leadership capabilities?

Describe a situation in which you took the initiative to lead or encourage others to actively experiment with new and different approaches to solving problems in your organization. What actions did you take? What outcomes were achieved? What did you learn as a result?

Think of a work challenge/assignment you face today. How can you actively experiment with new or different approaches while pursuing this challenge/assignment?

10. Closely Observe and Learn From Others

"…you need to have all your antennas, radar, everything alert, so you can learn, and then from there on you understand the dynamics so you just move on. But, it's a process of yourself learning, observing, understanding, and talking to people to . . . link all those points together."

Global Executive, How Global Leaders Develop, 2010

Introduction

Observing and learning from others is an important source of learning and development for leaders. Of course, as you doubtless already knew, leaders learn through a variety of diverse, challenging experiences, formal training and development, assignments, hardships, and other events. But observing and learning from others is a unique way to grow and develop, because it is "up close and personal." If you become expert at observing, reflecting, and maintaining a Learning Mindset you will discover that learning is all around you, all day – it just requires that you pay attention.

Review the list of behaviors, behavioral trends and patterns, and tendencies below. As you do, reflect on your own experience and try to recall specific situations or events that shed light on your own patterns of behavior related to this Learning Practice.

BEHAVIORS, BEHAVIORAL TRENDS AND PATTERNS, TENDENCIES:

- Train yourself to become a better observer
- Seek out someone who is known to be an expert at something you would like to learn about, and interview them about how they learned it themselves
- Identify someone who has a Learning Mindset, and who uses many of the Learning Practices, and ask them about their learning journey, how they developed their skills at learning from experience
- Work with a small group of leaders to learn from them and build a supportive social network that provides both motivation and accountability for learning

Potential Developmental Actions

Review the following for examples of developmental actions you can take to enhance your effectiveness at observing and learning from others. Identify at least one action that you will work to integrate into your day-to-day work life.

TRAIN YOURSELF TO BECOME A BETTER OBSERVER:

- When you are a skilled observer of people and situations, you are able to glean more – and more valuable – information about people and situations using one or more senses. Being able to observe with all of your senses enables you to communicate more effectively, make better decisions, and enhances your ability to interact with people. Observation, of people, objects, relationships between people, group dynamics, decision making, organizational climate, almost everything, is fundamental to learning from experience. The more you are skilled at observation, the more information you will be able to use to understand people and situations accurately.

- To improve your observation skills, engage in one or more of the following learning activities.
    - "Improving Observation Skills" – This is an internet-moderated case study with activities included. It's interesting, engaging, and packed with great resources, and can be used by anyone. There is no cost associated with the activity. You can access it at https://ccmit.mit.edu/observation/. Be sure to check out the Resources and Acknowledgements link where you can access even more help on improving your observation skills (https://ccmit.mit.edu/resources-and-acknowledgments/).
    - Another valuable resource on "How to be a good observer" can be found at the wikiHow website, https://www.wikihow.com/Be-a-Good-Observer. Two methods are highlighted: learning the habits of a good observer, and practicing your observation skills.

SEEK OUT SOMEONE WHO IS KNOWN TO BE AN EXPERT AT SOMETHING YOU WOULD LIKE TO LEARN ABOUT, AND INTERVIEW THEM ABOUT HOW THEY LEARNED IT THEMSELVES:

- Set a goal and write it down. Then, plan the interview using the following tips:
  - Share your goal with the expert and tell them that you view them as an expert on the topic of interest; ask them if they believe they possess the specific expertise and knowledge you would like to gain, and if they would share their expertise with you.
  - Prior to the interview, share the questions you would like to ask them.
  - When conducting the interview, restate the purpose and amount of time agreed for the interview.
  - Ask the expert specifically how they learned and developed their current level of expertise.
  - Take detailed notes, so that you can review them later to reflect on.
  - Try to avoid providing your own significant commentary during the interview. Emphasize questions to clarify, deepen, or expand on their remarks.
  - Be sure to use good interview skills, including stating the purpose, checking to make sure how much time they have for the interview, making eye contact, listening intently and actively, and demonstrating attentive body language.
  - Thank them at the end of the scheduled time and send them a thank you note shortly after the interview.

IDENTIFY SOMEONE WHO HAS A LEARNING MINDSET, AND WHO USES MANY OF THE LEARNING PRACTICES, AND ASK THEM ABOUT THEIR LEARNING JOURNEY, HOW THEY DEVELOPED THEIR SKILLS AT LEARNING FROM EXPERIENCE:

- Who do you know who seems to be a true "life-long learner," who is always learning? Someone who – every time you see them – has just read a great new book, is enrolled in another course at the local university, who is genuinely excited to discuss ideas with an open mind? It's a good chance that these are indicators of someone who has a learning mindset.

- You can use the checklist on the following page to identify someone who has a Learning Mindset, or you can use the Learning Mindset Questionnaire (in the Resources section of this Guide). How many of the six Learning Mindset elements have you seen evidence of in this person's life?

Learning Mindset Checklist

Use this checklist to identify someone who has a Learning Mindset. Review the list below and mark an "X" beside each item that you believe is true about a specific individual.

Based on my observations of this person's behaviors and actions, s/he . . .

1.	Is open to new experiences and ideas
2.	Is intellectually curious, and has broad interests
3.	Is receptive and open to change
4.	Is able to significantly grow and develop his/her knowledge, skills, and abilities
5.	Believes s/he can substantially change how much talent s/he has
6.	Is always striving to gain new knowledge, develop new skills, and improve my abilities
7.	Has a strong internal drive and desire to learn, grow, and develop
8.	Constantly seeks out and engages in new experiences in order to gain new knowledge and skills
9.	Enjoys the challenge and novelty of new experiences
10.	Feels a powerful inner need to learn about people in other companies and other parts of the world
11.	Has a strong desire to understand the challenges others face and how they deal with the challenges
12.	Is always searching for deeper understanding about the unique ways people in diverse settings and situations (e.g., roles, organizations, cultures) behave
13.	Frequently seeks out new, different situations in order to learn something new
14.	Often strikes out into unfamiliar territory just for the adventure and enjoyment of experiencing something different
15.	Frequently discards old habits of mind and perceptions in order to view experiences with a fresh perspective
16.	Acts with purpose and intention to learn something from every experience he/she has
17.	Even when an experience appears to be "negative" s/he searches for meaning and value in the experience
18.	Typically looks at unsatisfying/difficult situations as opportunities to gain valuable lessons and insights from experience

Checklist Item Key

Statement #	Dimension
1 – 3	Openness to Experience
4 – 6	Belief in Own Learning and Growth Potential
7 – 9	Motivated, Willing, and Desire to Learn
10 – 12	Curious About Others
13 – 15	Attitude of Discovery and Exploration
16 – 18	Intention and Willingness to Gain Something Positive From Experience

NOTE: If you marked an "X" beside all or most of the 18 items, this person very likely has a strong Learning Mindset. It could be very useful for you to speak with them about their approach to learning from experience, so that you can enhance your own Learning Mindset.

- Next, review the Learning Practices Survey (in the Resources section of this Guide), thinking about the individual you may want to interview. How many of the Learning Practices have you seen them demonstrate?

- After using these two tools to informally determine if this individual is truly a "lifelong learner" with a Learning Mindset, ask if you could interview them to learn from their experience. Set a date and agree on the amount of time they can meet with you, and ensure you will meet in a quiet location where there will be limited or no interruptions.

- A sample interview guide is provided below:
  - Prepare for the Interview
    - Confirm the interview date, time, location, and purpose with the individual you will interview.
    - Review your interview questions, and try to think of a couple of follow-up questions. Some sample interview questions are provided below.
    - Print a copy of the interview questions in advance, to take with you to the interview. You don't want to try to rely on your memory alone in a meeting like this!
    - You may want to send an advance copy of the interview questions to the person you're interviewing, and ask them to review them prior to the interview. However, some people infer that you want them to answer the questions in writing. This is undesirable because, while the answers may be more complete and polished, spontaneous answers may be more informative due to the fact that they may reveal more emotion and context than answers where they have had time to write and edit their responses. If you do send an advance copy of the interview questions, make sure they know they don't need to respond in writing. You could avoid this issue by

only confirming the purpose of the interview in advance, not sending the actual questions.

- o Conduct the Interview
  - Reconfirm the purpose of the meeting and the amount of time the individual has available.
  - Use your interview questions to guide the process. Some sample questions include:
    - What experiences have you had that were very important and significant in your development as a leader?
    - What lessons did you learn from those experiences? What insights did you gain from them?
    - How did you go about learning from your experiences? What, specifically, did you do to gain the learning from those experiences?
      - o For example, did you use a Learning Journal, participate in a Learning Circle or Peer Coaching group, regular individual reflection, or some other learning tactic?
  - Be attentive to the answers, and take detailed notes.
  - Ask follow-up questions to clarify something you didn't understand, or to have them elaborate on an answer or topic.
  - Gently re-direct the interview if the individual goes off-topic.
  - Conclude the interview on time. Thank the individual for the time and for sharing their experiences with you.
- o Follow Up
  - Write a short note or email thanking the individual for sharing their experiences with you.

WORK WITH A SMALL GROUP OF LEADERS TO LEARN FROM THEM AND BUILD A SUPPORTIVE SOCIAL NETWORK THAT PROVIDES BOTH MOTIVATION AND ACCOUNTABILITY FOR LEARNING:

- Learning Circles and Peer Coaching Groups offer leaders opportunities to explore problems and challenges they face with their colleagues and peers. "In a typical learning circle, a small group of six to eight leaders meets regularly (either face-to-face or virtually) to discuss the top challenges they are facing, how they are approaching these challenges, and what they are learning from their experience. They obtain feedback and coaching suggestions from other learning circle participants. Learning circles require leaders to articulate how they are thinking about their toughest problems, describe the approaches they have tried, reflect on what worked and didn't, and explore ways they can refine their approach. The reflection and after-action review that takes place in learning circles significantly enhances learning."[19]
  - To learn more about Learning Circles and Peer Coaching Groups contact us at steve@aspireconsulting.net.
- Like Learning Circles and Peer Coaching Groups, Action Learning programs also typically involve a small group of leaders who meet regularly, preferably face-to-face to discuss challenges and problems they are facing. Action Learning is "both a process and a powerful program that involves a small group of people solving real problems while at the same time focusing on what they are learning and how their learning can benefit each group member and the organization as a whole."[20] Action Learning programs include a designated group facilitator who monitors and manages the group's process and progress, intervening only to ensure the group stays focused and productive. Leaders who participate in Action Learning programs use a specific process of questioning, reflecting, deciding, and committing to learning that powerfully develops and improves leadership capabilities in the context of their job and organization.
  - To learn more about Action Learning programs, contact us at steve@aspireconsulting.net.

---

[19] Using Experience to Develop Leadership Talent. Cynthia D. McCauley and Morgan W. McCall. Jossey-Bass, 2014.
[20] Action Learning in Action. Michael J. Marquardt. Davies-Black, 1999.

Self-Assessment: Score Yourself on Observing and Learning from Others

Think about your work and life experiences over the past year and answer the following questions using this scale:

Never (1)   Rarely (2)   Sometimes (3)   Often (4)   Almost always (5)

- I train myself to become a better observer.   **1   2   3   4   5**

- I seek out people who are experts at things I would like to learn   **1   2   3   4   5**
  about and interview them about how they learned it themselves.

- I identify someone who has a Learning Mindset, and who uses many   **1   2   3   4   5**
  of the Learning Practices, and ask them about their learning
  journey, how they developed their skills at learning from
  experience.

- I work with a small group of leaders to learn from them and build a   **1   2   3   4   5**
  supportive social network that provides both motivation and
  accountability for learning.

OVERALL SCORE:
Sum of Ratings divided by 5 (Number of Items)

Guide to Interpreting Your Overall Score

- If your overall score on this learning practice is 12 or less, this is a good time to work on observing and learning from others. Think about a skill you want to improve on that you could learn by observing others. Then, work through various ways to observe some experts and learn from them. Are you a good observer? How could you improve? What can you do to change your own and others' perceptions that you need to improve in this area? Refer to the Potential Developmental Actions for ideas on how you can become a better listener.

- If your overall score on this learning practice is 13 to 17, you are already using it to learn, by observing others. How can you turn this into one of your strongest learning practices? What can you do to develop a reputation as someone who others want to observe and learn from? What is one thing you need to do to turn this into one of your core capabilities? Review the Potential Developmental Actions for ideas on how you can listen more effectively.

- If your overall score on this learning practice is 18 or above, congratulations! You are actively engaged in observing and learning from others. Think about how you can help others improve in this learning practice.

REFLECTION QUESTIONS

How have you learned, grown, and/or developed as a leader as a result of observing someone else? Who did you observe, and how did you do that? What did you learn from observing that person?

Think of someone you would like to "shadow" or observe in order to learn, grow and develop. What would you like to gain by observing them? How can you make that happen?

How have you learned, grown, or developed as a leader as a result of observing someone you consider to be a "bad example"? Who did you observe and how did you do that? What did you learn from observing that person?

What is one your main challenges with learning by observing others?

What is your plan to put this learning practice into action going forward? How will you know you are successful?

TOOLS & RESOURCES

LEARNING MINDSET

THE LEARNING MINDSET MODEL

The following list of the Learning Mindset model's six dimensions and their descriptors summarizes key aspects of the model.

1. **Open to Experience**
   - Open to new experiences and ideas
   - Intellectually curious and have broad interests
   - Receptive and open to change

2. **Motivated, Willing and Desire to Change**
   - Strong internal drive and desire to learn, grow, and develop
   - Constantly seek out and engage in new experiences in order to gain new knowledge and skills
   - Enjoy the challenge and novelty of new experiences

3. **Curious About Others**
   - Feel a powerful inner need to learn about people in other countries and other parts of the world
   - Have a strong desire to understand the challenges other face and how they deal with the challenges
   - Always searching for deeper understanding about the unique ways people in diverse settings and situations (e.g. roles, organizations, cultures) behave

4. **Attitude of Discovery and Exploration**
   - Frequently seek out new, different situations in order to learn something new
   - Often strike out into unfamiliar territory just for the adventure and enjoyment of experiencing something different
   - Frequently discard old habits of mind and perceptions in order to view experiences with a fresh perspective

5. **Intention and Willingness to Gain Something Positive from Experience**
   - Act with purpose and intention to learn something from every experience I have
   - Even when an experience appears to be "negative" I search for meaning and value in the experience
   - Typically look at unsatisfying/difficult situations as opportunities to gain valuable lessons and insights from experience

6. **Belief in My Own Learning and Growth Potential**
   - Believe I am able to significantly grow and develop my knowledge, skills, and abilities
   - Believe I can substantially change how much talent I have
   - Always striving to gain new knowledge, develop new skills, and improve my abilities

Learning Mindset Questionnaire (LMQ)

Learning from experience is a critical skill for leaders. It requires a **Learning Mindset**, which is an **_attitude_** toward learning that predisposes you to be open to new experiences, to believe you can and will learn, and to intentionally grow and develop from your experience. A Learning Mindset leads to the consistent, rigorous practice of certain learning-oriented **_actions_** – **Learning Practices** – that in turn result in learning more from experience, faster, while achieving better results.

Learning Practices are **Actions** you can take to accelerate your learning from experience. Your actions determine whether you proactively pursue learning in your day-to-day work life, or focus only on getting the job done. Leaders who consistently and rigorously use the Learning Practices in their day-to-day work life learn significantly more, faster while achieving better results.

> *If you adopt and sustain The Learning Mindset, and consistently and rigorously employ certain Learning Practices, you will learn significantly more from experience, faster. As a result, you will perform at a higher level and increase your potential to take on more significant challenges in the future.*

The **Learning Mindset Questionnaire** provides you with an opportunity to evaluate your own attitude toward learning from experience. The companion self-assessment, The **Learning Practices Survey** is a self-assessment tool that enables you to assess your current use of these learning practices, which in turn helps you to identify opportunities to improve your ability to learn from experience. Because the two tools complement each other, you will develop a more comprehensive understanding of your ability to learn from experience by completing both assessments.

As with any self-assessment tool, getting useful results depend on you answering the questions honestly, without any attempt to create a certain kind of impression. You will gain the most from this tool by reading each question carefully and responding candidly, and then using the assessment results to identify your greatest opportunities to learn, grow, and develop based on the survey results.

Learning Mindset Questionnaire (LMQ)

This questionnaire consists of 18 statements. Please indicate how much you agree or disagree with each statement by checking the rating that corresponds to your belief/point of view.

	Strongly Disagree	Mostly Disagree	Slightly Disagree	Slightly Agree	Mostly Agree	Strongly Agree
	0	1	2	3	4	5
1. I am open to new experiences and ideas	☐	☐	☐	☐	☐	☐
2. I am intellectually curious, and has broad interests	☐	☐	☐	☐	☐	☐
3. I am receptive and open to change	☐	☐	☐	☐	☐	☐
4. I am able to significantly grow and develop my knowledge, skills, and abilities	☐	☐	☐	☐	☐	☐
5. I can substantially change how much talent I have	☐	☐	☐	☐	☐	☐
6. I am always striving to gain new knowledge, develop new skills, and improve my abilities	☐	☐	☐	☐	☐	☐
7. I have a strong internal drive and desire to learn, grow, and develop	☐	☐	☐	☐	☐	☐
8. I constantly seek out and engage in new experiences in order to gain new knowledge and skills	☐	☐	☐	☐	☐	☐
9. I enjoy the challenge and novelty of new experiences	☐	☐	☐	☐	☐	☐
10. I feel a powerful inner need to learn about people in other companies and other parts of the world	☐	☐	☐	☐	☐	☐
11. I have a strong desire to understand the challenges others face and how they deal with the challenges	☐	☐	☐	☐	☐	☐
12. I am always searching for deeper understanding about the unique ways people in diverse settings and situations (e.g., roles, organizations, cultures) behave	☐	☐	☐	☐	☐	☐
13. I frequently seek out new, different situations in order to learn something new	☐	☐	☐	☐	☐	☐
14. I often strike out into unfamiliar territory just for the adventure and enjoyment of experiencing something different	☐	☐	☐	☐	☐	☐
15. I frequently discard old habits of mind and perceptions in order to view experiences with a fresh perspective	☐	☐	☐	☐	☐	☐
16. I act with purpose and intention to learn something from every experience I have	☐	☐	☐	☐	☐	☐
17. Even when an experience appears to be "negative" I search for meaning and value in the experience	☐	☐	☐	☐	☐	☐
18. I typically look at unsatisfying/difficult situations as opportunities to gain valuable lessons and insights from experience	☐	☐	☐	☐	☐	☐

Learning Mindset Questionnaire (LMQ)

Scoring Instructions:

1. Add your ratings for the following groups of statements, and find the average rating for each group. Write the average rating in the space provided below. Then, add the averages together, and find the overall average rating for all six dimensions.

Statement #	Sum	Average Rating	Dimension
1 – 3			Openness to Experience
4 – 6			Belief in Own Learning and Growth Potential
7 – 9			Motivated, Willing, and Desire to Learn
10 – 12			Curious About Others
13 – 15			Attitude of Discovery and Exploration
16 – 18			Intention and Willingness to Gain Something Positive From Experience
Sum of All 6			**Overall Average Rating**

2. In the blank chart below, write an "X" or draw a bar to indicate your average rating for each Learning Mindset Dimension.

Ratings		Open to Exp.	Growth Potential	Motivated to Learn	Curious	Discover & Explore	Intentional
	5						
	4.5						
	4						
	3.5						
	3						
	2.5						
	2						
	1.5						
	1						
	.5						
	0						

Learning Mindset Questionnaire (LMQ)

Interpreting Your LMQ Score:

This guide to interpreting your LMQ score is provided to help you gauge how much you possess an attitude toward learning that predisposes you to be open to new experiences, to believe you can and will learn, and to intentionally grow and develop from your experience. The questionnaire may enable you to identify opportunities to adopt or modify your attitude toward learning in ways that increase your ability to learn from experience and elevate your performance and potential as a result. Use these results to identify how your beliefs and attitudes about yourself and learning are impacting your ability to learn from experience.

Overall Average Rating Range	Interpretation
4.5 – 5.0	**Strong:** You "Strongly Agree" with most of the 18 statements that describe the 6 dimensions of the Learning Mindset. This indicates that you probably have a strong Learning Mindset. You are probably very open to new experiences, believe you can and will learn from most experiences, and you intentionally grow and develop from your experience.
3.5 – 4.4	**Moderate:** Your ratings indicate that you "Mostly Agree" with quite a few of the 18 statements that describe the 6 dimensions of the Learning Mindset, and you probably rated some of the statements as a "5" or "Strongly Agree." However, you also rated some of the statements as "3" or Slightly Agree. This indicates that you probably have a moderately strong Learning Mindset. You may want to review your ratings to discover if any of the 6 dimensions are rated relatively lower than the others, in order to understand where you have an opportunity for further growth and development.
3.4 or lower	**Opportunity:** Your ratings indicate that, overall, you "Slightly Agree" with the 18 statements that describe the 6 dimensions of the Learning Mindset. It's likely that you rated several of the statements as a "3" or lower. This indicates that you have a real opportunity to increase your Learning Mindset. Review your ratings to discover if any of the 6 dimensions are rated relatively lower than the others, in order to understand where you have an opportunity for further growth and development.

For support in developing your Learning Mindset, contact Aspire Consulting: steve@aspireconsulting.net or 757-647-2571.

LEARNING PRACTICES

TEN LEARNING PRACTICES

1. **Take responsibility for your own learning and development**
   - Feel personally accountable to actively pursue your own professional growth and development
   - Take the initiative to improve your leadership capabilities
   - Develop goals and action plans to improve your knowledge and/or abilities related to your job or career
   - Intentionally reframe your experiences to view them as learning opportunities
   - Look for ways to learn something new while pursuing your work goals, assignments, and projects
   - Persistently work through difficult issues and overcome obstacles to accomplish desired changes

2. **Approach new assignments/opportunities with openness to experience and positive intention to learn**
   - Automatically think to yourself when you have a new assignment, "This is a great opportunity to learn something new"
   - Welcome assignments to projects or tasks that you have never done before
   - Look forward to different types of experiences because of the learning you might gain
   - Find something useful to learn in most experiences
   - Intentionally look for something to learn, even when an experience is difficult, challenging, or not to your liking

3. **Seek and use feedback**
   - Ask colleagues (such as your direct manager/supervisor, peers, customers, stakeholders, and/or direct reports) for feedback about your performance, behaviors, and/or competencies
   - Listen closely to the feedback you receive
   - Follow up with and thank your colleagues for giving you useful feedback
   - Listen closely to what might NOT be said (behind the words)
   - Take feedback, both positive and constructive, to heart and do your best to use it to change, grow and develop

4. **Develop a clear understanding of your strengths and areas of development**
   - Take stock of your personality characteristics, and how they influence your performance and behavior at work
   - Assess yourself against the leadership competencies in the competency model of your organization
   - Ask others to help you by sharing their perspective on your strengths and areas for further development
   - Identify your top strengths and top areas for further development

5. **Ask great questions and demonstrate curiosity**
   - Ask open-ended questions to encourage people to expand their ideas and share them with you
   - Ask probing questions in order to learn more about something
   - Frame your questions positively
   - Ask questions from the Learning Mindset, seeking to learn rather than to judge

6. **Listen transformatively**
   - Listen to others with the Learning Mindset, seeking to learn rather than to judge
   - Listen to explore your own perceptions, filters, and biases, and become aware of how they affect your behavior
   - Listen intently, deeply, empathically
   - Listen to understand both the content and the affect of the speaker
   - Listen to grasp the intentions and deeper purpose of the speaker, i.e., what they want to achieve

7. **Respond to experience with adaptability and flexibility**
   - Change your behavior according to the situation at hand
   - Resist the tendency to use "muscle memory" (old, familiar ways of leading and acting) and proactively choose my actions depending on the circumstance
   - Not insisting on your own way, even when you have "been there, done that" and think you know the "right" way
   - Soliciting others' ideas about how to handle situations, especially those from different cultural backgrounds and life experiences

8. **Actively reflect / Practice mindfulness**
   - Take the time to reflect on and think about situations you have been in at work, what your behavior was, how you were feeling, what the outcome was, and any insight or lesson you gained
   - Actively reflect during situations, so that you self-direct or self-correct and make changes to your behavior or words that bring about a more desirable outcome
   - Reflect with others to gain an appreciation for their perspective and to broaden your awareness
   - Maintain a high degree of awareness of the people, actions, interactions, and dynamics around you, in order to make sense of situations and experiences as they occur
   - Pay attention to the present moment; watch your thoughts with detachment and without judgment

9. **Actively experiment with new approaches to learning**
   - Frequently try different approaches to solving problems
   - Play around with different ways of presenting an idea you have
   - Brainstorm with colleagues new ways of doing what you have done for years

10. **Observe and learn from others**
    - Train yourself to become a better observer
    - Seek out someone who is known to be an expert at something you want to learn about, and interview them about how they learned it themselves
    - Identify someone who has a Learning Mindset and who uses many of the Learning Practices; ask them about their learning journey and how they developed their skills at learning from experience
    - Identify someone who is recognized as an outstanding leader or specialist, and "shadow" them to learn first-hand how they do what they do; interview them to learn more
    - Work with a small group of leaders to learn from them and build a supportive social network that provides both motivation and accountability for learning

Learning Practices Survey (LPS)

Learning from experience is a critical skill for leaders. It requires a **Learning Mindset**, which is an **_attitude_** toward learning that predisposes you to be open to new experiences, to believe you can and will learn, and to intentionally grow and develop from your experience. A Learning Mindset leads to the consistent, rigorous practice of certain learning-oriented **_actions_** – **Learning Practices** – that in turn result in learning more from experience, faster, while achieving better results.

Learning Practices are **Actions** you can take to accelerate your learning from experience. Your actions determine whether you proactively pursue learning in your day-to-day work life, or focus only on getting the job done. Leaders who consistently and rigorously use the Learning Practices in their day-to-day work life learn significantly more, faster while achieving better results.

> *If you adopt and sustain The Learning Mindset, and consistently and rigorously employ certain Learning Practices, you will learn significantly more from experience, faster. As a result, you will perform at a higher level and increase your potential to take on more significant challenges in the future.*

The **Learning Practices Survey** is a self-assessment tool that enables you to assess your current use of these learning practices, which in turn helps you to identify opportunities to improve your ability to learn from experience. The companion self-assessment, the **Learning Mindset Questionnaire**, provides you with an opportunity to evaluate your own attitude toward learning from experience. Because the two tools complement each other, you may develop a more comprehensive understanding of your ability to learn from experience by completing both assessments.

As with any self-assessment tool, getting useful results depend on you answering the questions honestly, without any attempt to create a certain kind of impression. You will gain the most from this tool by reading each question carefully and responding candidly, and then using the assessment results to identify your greatest opportunities to learn, grow, and develop based on the survey results.

Learning Practices Survey (LPS)

Mark an "X" in the appropriate box to indicate the frequency with which you use each of the 10 Learning Practices, actions that you take on the job to promote your own learning and development. Bullet points in italics provide descriptors of each practice.

How often do you….	Never	Rarely	Sometimes	Often	Always
1. Take responsibility for your own learning and development • *Feel personally accountable to actively pursue your own professional growth and development* • *Take the initiative to improve your leadership capabilities* • *Develop goals and action plans to improve your knowledge and/or abilities related to your job or career* • *Intentionally reframe your experiences to view them as learning opportunities* • *Look for ways to learn something new while pursuing your work goals, assignments, and projects* • *Persistently work through difficult issues and overcome obstacles to accomplished desired changes*					
2. Approach new assignments/opportunities with openness to experience and positive intention to learn • *Automatically think to yourself when you have a new assignment, "This is a great opportunity to learn something new"* • *Welcome assignments to projects or tasks that you have never done before* • *Look forward to different types of experiences because of the learning you might gain* • *Find something useful to learn in most experiences* • *Intentionally look for something to learn, even when an experience is difficult, challenging, or not to your liking*					
3. Seek and use feedback • *Ask colleagues (e.g., your direct manager, peers, customers, stakeholders, and/or direct reports) for feedback about your performance, behaviors, and/or competencies* • *Listen closely to the feedback that others give you* • *Listen closely to what might NOT be said (behind the words)* • *Follow up with and thank your colleagues for giving you useful feedback* • *Take feedback, both positive and constructive, to heart and do your best to use it to change, grow and develop*					

Learning Practices Survey (LPS)

How often do you….	Never	Rarely	Sometimes	Often	Always
4. Develop a clear understanding of your strengths and areas of development • *Take stock of your personality characteristics, and how they influence your performance and behavior at work* • *Assess yourself against the leadership competencies in the competency model of your organization* • *Ask others to help you by sharing their perspective on your strengths and areas for further development* • *Identify your top strengths and top areas for further development*					
5. Ask great questions and demonstrate curiosity • *Ask open-ended questions to encourage people to expand their ideas and share them with you* • *Ask probing questions in order to learn more about something* • *Frame your questions positively* • *Ask questions from the Learning Mindset, seeking to learn rather than to judge*					
6. Listen transformatively • *Listen to others with the Learning Mindset, seeking to learn rather than to judge* • *Listen to explore your own perceptions, filters, and biases, and become aware of how they affect your behavior* • *Listen intently, deeply, empathically* • *Listen to understand both the content and the affect/emotions of the speaker* • *Listen to grasp the intentions and deeper purpose of the speaker, i.e., what they want to achieve*					
7. Respond to experience with adaptability and flexibility • *Change your behavior according to the situation at hand* • *Resist the tendency to use old, familiar ways of leading and proactively choose my actions depending on the circumstance* • *Not insisting on your own way, even when you have "been there, done that" and think you know the "right" way* • *Soliciting others' ideas about how to handle situations, especially those from different cultural backgrounds*					

Learning Practices Survey (LPS)

How often do you….	Never	Rarely	Sometimes	Often	Always
8. Actively reflect and demonstrate mindfulness					
• *Take the time to reflect on and think about situations you have been in at work, what your behavior was, how you were feeling, what the outcome was, and any insight or lesson you gained*					
• *Actively reflect during situations, so that you self-direct or self-correct and make changes to your behavior or words that bring about a more desirable outcome*					
• *Reflect with others to gain an appreciation for their perspective and to broaden your awareness*					
• *Maintain a high degree of awareness of the people, actions, interactions, and dynamics around you, in order to make sense of situations and experiences as they occur*					
• *Pay attention to the present moment; watch your thoughts with detachment and without judgment*					
9. Actively experiment with new approaches					
• *Frequently try different approaches to solving problems*					
• *Play around with different ways of presenting an idea you have*					
• *Brainstorm with colleagues new ways of doing what you have done for years*					
10. Observe and learn from others					
• *Train yourself to become a better observer*					
• *Seek out someone who is known to be an expert at something you want to learn about; interview them about how they learned it themselves; closely watch what they do and how they do it*					
• *Identify someone who has a Learning Mindset, and who uses many of the Learning Practices, and ask them about their learning journey, how they developed their skills at "learning from experience"*					
• *Work with a small group of leaders to learn from them and build a supportive social network that provides both motivation and accountability for learning*					

LPS Scoring Instructions

Two activities are provided to help you make the most of your LPS self-assessment: Rank Order and Overall LPS Score.

Rank Order Your LPS Ratings

Review the ratings you gave for each of the ten Learning Practices, and list them below in order from **Most Often** to **Least Often**. It's important to include those practices that you use frequently so that you keep their importance in mind and continue using them to learn from your experience. But it's also important to notice those Learning Practices that you use least frequently, or not at all, so that you become aware of the specific behaviors you can use more, to increase your learning from experience.

Frequency	#	Learning Practices
Most Often		
Least Often		

Overall LPS Score

Scoring Instructions:

1. Transfer your ratings for each of the ten Learning Practices into the table below. For example, if you rated Learning Practice #1 a "5" (Always), mark an "X" under the "Always / 5" column in the first row.

2. Add the number of X's for each rating column (e.g., "Never," "Rarely," etc.). Write the total number for each column in the TOTAL row. For example, if you have 4 X's in the "Always / 5" column, you would write "4" in that column, in the shaded TOTAL cell.

3. Next, multiply the TOTAL for each column and write the product in the POINTS cell for each column. For example, if you have a total of "4" under column 5, multiply it times 5 and write the product (20) under that column in the shaded POINTS cell.

4. Add all of the points in the POINTS row of cells. Note that the columns titled "Never / 1" and "Rarely / 2" receive no points ("0"), so you will total the points from columns 3, 4, and 5, and write the total in the box labeled TOTAL LPS SCORE.

Learning Practices	Never 1	Rarely 2	Sometimes 3	Often 4	Always 5
1. Take responsibility for your own learning and development					
2. Approach new assignments with openness to experience					
3. Seek and use feedback					
4. Develop a clear understanding of your strengths & dev. needs					
5. Ask great questions and demonstrate curiosity					
6. Listen transformatively					
7. Respond to experience with adaptability and flexibility					
8. Actively reflect and demonstrate mindfulness					
9. Actively experiment with new approaches					
10. Observe and learn from others					
TOTAL					
MULTIPLY X	0	0	3	4	5
POINTS	0	0			

TOTAL LPS SCORE [   ]

Interpreting Your LPS Score:

Score Range	Interpretation
45 – 50	**Strong:** You always or often use most of the Learning Practices to learn from experience. You proactively pursue learning in your day-to-day work life, and blend learning with getting the job done. As you consistently, intentionally, and rigorously use the Learning Practices, you are highly likely to learn a great deal from experience. If your ratings are accurate, they indicate that you have a strong Learning Mindset.
35 – 44	**Moderate:** You often or always use some of the Learning Practices to learn from experience. You may tend to use some Learning Practices more than others. You may tend to focus a bit more on getting the job done more than learning from your experience. You could improve your ability to learn from experience by using more Learning Practices more consistently, intentionally, and rigorously. If your ratings are accurate, they indicate that you have a moderately strong Learning Mindset.
34 or lower	**Opportunity:** You infrequently and/or inconsistently use some of the Learning Practices to learn from experience. You may rely on a few of the Learning Practices much more than others. You probably focus more on producing results than on learning while producing results. You have a real opportunity to significantly improve your ability to learn from experience, by using more Learning Practices more consistently, intentionally, and rigorously. If you do this, you will learn more, faster, and as a result you will perform at a higher level and create greater value for yourself and your company. You may want to evaluate your Learning Mindset to identify how your beliefs and attitudes about yourself and learning are impacting your ability to learn from experience. You may also want to develop a stronger Learning Mindset.

Please note that these scores and interpretations are only broad guides to assist you in gaining a better understanding of your active, intentional learning from experience. Use the activities on the following pages to gain the true value from the self-assessment.

TAKING ACTION TO LEARN MORE FROM EXPERIENCE

Now that you have scored your LPS, you have a much better understanding of how often you use the ten Learning Practices on a day-to-day basis. Use this information to identify ways you can improve your ability to learn from experience. Learning from experience almost never comes through a direct path, where you have an experience and then at the end the new learning is just somehow "there" in your mind. Learning from experience more often comes through a circuitous route, filled with trials and errors, dead ends, frustration, and starting over. Experience is almost always beyond our control; what we can control is whether and how we prepare for an experience, how we respond to and take action during an experience, and whether and how we actively reflect on and take other steps to squeeze the most learning from an experience. The following 3-step process will help you develop a plan of action to learn more from experience. A partially completed example Development Action Plan is provided on the following pages to guide you as you develop your own Action Plan.

1 - **Identify Learning Practices to Work On.** First, review your Rank Order list of the ten Learning Practices to identify one or two practices that you want to use more frequently to learn more from experience. You might select the two practices that you have been using least often, or you could also choose Learning Practices that fall somewhere in the middle of the rank order. It's less important to focus on the two least frequently used practices than it is to be interested and motivated enough to put the practices you select into action. Now, list the two Learning Practices you want to use more often in the appropriate column below. For example, you might list *"Take responsibility for my own learning and development"* as a Learning Practice to work on.

2 - **Select Behaviors, Behavioral Trends and Patterns, and Tendencies.** Next, review the following section of this Guide to identify one or two Behaviors, Behavioral Trends and Patterns, and Tendencies that you want to work on. For example, you might list *"Hold myself personally accountable to actively pursue my own professional growth and development"* as a Behavior to focus on. List the items you choose in the spaces provided in the table below.

3 - **Specify Development Actions.** Review the list of Recommended Development Actions (pages 20 and following). Identify one or two Development Actions you plan to take to improve your ability to learn from experience. For example, if you chose the specific behavior *"Hold yourself personally accountable to actively pursue your own professional growth and development,"* you could choose to implement one or two of the four actions listed. For example, you could choose the first Development Action from the list below: *"Review your work calendar/schedule to identify how much time you invest every week into your own learning, growth, or development . . ."* List the Development Actions you plan to implement in the Development Action Plan provided on the next page.

Development Action Plan - EXAMPLE

Rank #	**1** - Learning Practices	**2** - Behaviors, Behavioral Trends and Patterns, and Tendencies	**3** - Development Actions
10	*Take responsibility for my own learning and development*	*Hold myself personally accountable to actively pursue my own professional growth and development*	• *Review my work calendar/schedule to identify how much time I invest every week into my own learning, growth, or development.* • *Set aside a specific amount of time each week on a specific day* • *Tell Joe about my commitment and ask him to help me be accountable by checking in with me every week*

My Development Action Plan

Rank #	**1** - Learning Practices	**2** - Behaviors, Behavioral Trends and Patterns, and Tendencies	**3** - Development Actions

Recommended Readings

- <u>Accelerating Your Development as a Leader</u>. Robert Barner, 2011, Pfeiffer.

- <u>Action Learning in Action</u>. Michael J. Marquardt, 1999. Davies-Black.

- *Brainstorming*. MindTools, <u>https://www.mindtools.com/brainstm.html.</u>

- <u>Change Your Questions, Change Your Life.</u> Marilee Adams, 2009, Berrett-Koehler.

- <u>Changing on the Job.</u> Jennifer Garvey Berger, 2012, Stanford Business Books.

- <u>The Communication Catalyst.</u> Mickey Connolly and Richard Rianoshek, 2002, Kaplan Publishing.

- *<u>Critical Reflections: How Groups Can Learn from Success and Failure.</u>* Chris Ernst and André Martin, 2011, Pfeiffer/Center for Creative Leadership.

- <u>Crucibles of Leadership: How to Learn From Experience to Become a Great Leader.</u> Robert Thomas, 2008, Harvard Business School Publishing.

- *The Executive's Guide to Better Listening.* Bernard T. Ferrari, 2012, McKinsey Quarterly.

- <u>Experiential Learning: Experience as the Source of Learning and Development</u>. 2015, Pearson Education.

- <u>Fully Present: The Science, Art, and Practice of Mindfulness.</u> Susan Smalley and Diana Winston, 2010, Da Capo.

- *The Future of Lifelong Learning – Designing for a Learning-Integrated Life.* D2L Corporation, 2020.

- <u>FYI For Learning Agility.</u> Robert Eichinger, Michael Lombardo, & Cara Capretta, 2010, Korn/Ferry International.

- *Global Leadership Development: What Global Organizations Can Do to Reduce Leadership Risk, Increase Speed to Competence, and Build Global Leadership Muscle.* Steve Terrell & Katherine Rosenbusch, People & Strategy, Vol. 36, Issue 1, 2013 (pp. 40 – 46)

- *How global leaders develop.* Steve Terrell & Katherine Rosenbusch, Journal of Management Development, Vol. 32, No. 10, 2013 (pp. 1056 – 1079)

- *How global leaders develop.* Terrell, UMI/Proquest, 2010.

- Innovative Leadership Workbook for Global Leaders. Maureen Metcalf, Steve Terrell, & Ben Mitchell, 2014, Integral Publishers.

- Leadership Agility: Five Levels of Mastery for Anticipating and Initiating Change. Bill Joiner and Stephen Josephs, 2007, Jossey-Bass.

- *Leadership experience and leader performance: Another hypothesis shot to hell.* Fiedler, F. E., Organizational Behavior and Human Performance (5), 1-14. (1970).

- *Leadership is a Contact Sport.* Marshall Goldsmith, http://www.marshallgoldsmith.com/articles/leadership-is-a-contact-sport-an-8-step-leadership-development-model-for-success/

- Leading with Questions. Michael Marquardt, 2005, Jossey-Bass.

- *Learn From Experience.* Steve Terrell, Leadership Excellence (*www.leaderexcel.com*), June, 2013.

- Learning Mindset for Leaders: Leveraging Experience to Accelerate Development. Steve Terrell, 2020, Independently Published.

- Lessons of Experience: How Successful Executives Develop on the Job. Michael McCall, Michael Lombardo, and Ann Morrison, 1988, Free Press.

- The Little Book of Talent: 52 Tips for Improving Your Skills. Daniel Coyle, 2012, Bantam Books.

- *Managerial Mindsets Research Project: Executive Summary.* L.A. Isabella and T. Forbes, Darden Graduate School of Business Administration, University of Virginia, Charlottesville, April 1994; and interview with the authors, 13 June 1994.

- Mindfulness. E. J. Langer, 1989, Addison-Wesley.

- On Being Certain: Believing You Are Right Even When You're Not. Robert Burton, 2008, St. Martin's Griffin.

- The Owner's Manual for Personality at Work. Pierce Howard and Jane Howard, 2001, Bard Press.

- The Power of Intention. Annie Murphy Paul, 2013, The Brilliant Blog (http://anniemurphypaul.com/blog/)

- The Power of Mindful Learning. E. J. Langer, 1997, Addison-Wesley.

- Practice Perfect: 42 Rules for Getting Better at Getting Better. Doug Lemov, Erica Woolway, and Katie Yezzi, 2012, Jossey-Bass.

- The Presentation Secrets of Steve Jobs. Carmine Gallo, 2010, McGraw Hill.

- Profit From Experience: A Handbook for Learning, Growth, and Change. Michael O'Brien and Larry Shook, 1995, Berkeley Books.

- Real-Time Leadership Development. Paul Yost and Mary Plunkett, 2009, Wiley-Blackwell.

- Talent is Overrated: What Really Separates World-Class Performers From Everybody Else. Geoff Colvin, 2010, Portfolio.

- The Talent Code: Greatness Isn't Born. It's Grown. Here's How. Daniel Coyle, 2009, Bantam Books.

- *Teaching Smart People How to Learn. Harvard Business Review, 69*(3), 99.

- <u>Thinking, Fast and Slow</u>. Farrar, 2001, Straus and Giroux.

- *To be a great leader, you need the right mindset.* Gottfredson & Reina, Harvard Business Review, Digital Article, January 17, 2020

- *Try FeedForward Instead of Feedback.* Marshall Goldsmith, The Talent Strategy Group, adapted from Leader to Leader, Summer 2002.

- <u>Using Experience to Develop Leadership Talent</u>. Cynthia D. McCauley and Morgan W. McCall, 2014, Jossey-Bass.

- *Virtuous circle and vicious circle.* Wikipedia, sourced January 30, 2020.

  https://en.wikipedia.org/wiki/Virtuous_circle_and_vicious_circle

- *Volatility, uncertainty, complexity, and ambiguity.* Wikipedia article, sourced January 30, 2020.

- <u>Work-Based Learning: The New Frontier of Management Development</u>. Joseph Raelin, 2000, Prentice Hall.

- *Why I'm a Listener: Amgen CEO Kevin Sharer.* McKinsey Quarterly, April 2012.

Academic Readings

Argyris, C. (1982). The Executive Mind and Double-Loop Learning. *Organizational Dynamics, 11*(2), 5-22.

Argyris, C. (1991). Teaching Smart People How to Learn. *Harvard Business Review, 69*(3), 99.

Barnett, B. G. (1989). *Reflection: The cornerstone of learning from experience*. Paper presented at the University Council for Educational Administrators Annual Convention.

Black, J. S. (2006). The mindset of global leaders: Inquisitiveness and duality. In W. H. Mobley (Ed.), *Advances in global leadership* (Vol. 4, pp. 181-200). Stamford, CT: JAI Press.

Boud, D., Keogh, R., & Walker, D. (Eds.). (1985). *Reflection: Turning experience into learning*. New York: Kogan Page.

Boud, D., & Walker, D. (1990). Making the most of experience. *Studies in Continuing Education, 12*(2).

Boyd, E. M., & Fales, A. W. (1983). Reflective learning: Key to learning from experience. *Journal of Humanistic Psychology, 23*(2), 99-117.

Candy, P. (1991). *Self-direction for lifelong learning* (2nd ed.). San Francisco: Jossey-Bass.

Cox, E. (2005). Adult learners learning from experience: using a reflective practice model to support work-based learning. *Reflective Practice, 6*(4), 459-472.

Dalton, M. A. (1998a). *Becoming a more versatile learner*. Greensboro: Center for Creative Leadership.

Daudelin, M. W. (1996). Learning from Experience Through Reflection. *Organizational Dynamics, 24*(3), 36-48.

Eichinger, R. W., & Lombardo, M. M. (2004). Learning Agility as a Prime Indicator of Potential. *HR. Human Resource Planning, 27*(4), 12.

Evans, C. (2000). *The lessons of experience: Developmental experiences of mid-level female administrators in higher education*. Unpublished Ed.D., Columbia University Teachers College, United States -- New York.

Kolb, D. A. (1984). *Experiential learning: Experience as the source of learning and development*. Englewood Cliffs: Prentice Hall.

Lombardo, M. M., & Eichinger, R. W. (1989). *Eighty-eight assignments for development in place.* Greensboro, NC: CCL Press.

Lombardo, M. M., & Eichinger, R. W. (2000). High potentials as high learners. *Human Resource Management, 39*(4), 321-329.

March, J. G. (2010). *The ambiguities of experience.* New York: Cornell University.

McCall, M. W., Jr. (1988). Developing Executives Through Work Experiences. *Human Resource Planning, 11*(1), 1.

McCall, M. W., Jr. (2004). Leadership development through experience. *Academy of Management Executive, 18*(3), 127-130.

McCall, M. W., Jr., & Hollenbeck, G. P. (2002). *Developing global executives: The lessons of international experience.* Boston: Harvard Business School Press.

McCall, M. W., Jr., Lombardo, M. M., & Morrison, A. M. (1988). *The lessons of experience.* Lexington, MA: Lexington Books (Free Press).

McCauley, C. D. (2006). *Developmental assignments: Creating learning experiences without changing jobs.* Greensboro, NC: Center for Creative Leadership.

Mumford, A. (1994). Four approaches to learning from experience. *The Learning Organization, 1*(1), 4-10.

Pietersen, W. G. (2002). *Reinventing strategy: Using strategic learning to create and sustain breakthrough performance.* New York: John Wiley & Sons.

Ruderman, M. N., & Ohlott, P. O. (2000). *Learning from life: Turning life's lessons into leadership experiences.* Greensboro: Center for Creative Leadership.

Schön, D. A. (1983). *The reflective practitioner: How professionals think in action.* New York: Basic Books.

Schön, D. A. (1987). *Educating the reflective practitioner.* San Francisco: John Wiley & Sons, Inc.

Terrell, R.S. (2014). *Learning Mindset: Developing Leaders Through Experience.* www.trainingmag.com (March, 2014)

Vaill, P. (1996). *Learning as a way of being.* San Francisco: Jossey-Bass.

Van Velsor, E., & Guthrie, V. A. (1998). Enhancing the ability to learn from experience. In C. McCauley, R. S. Moxley & E. Van Velsor (Eds.), *The Center for Creative Leadership handbook of leadership development* (pp. 242-261). San Francisco: Jossey-Bass.

Made in the USA
Las Vegas, NV
23 July 2021